MW00699266

BECOMING A BETTER MAN:

WHEN "SOMETHING'S GOTTA CHANGE" MAYBE IT'S YOU!

First Printing, 2019
ISBN 978-1-9992490-0-7
Mike Cameron
www.mikecameron.ca

For Uncle Johnny:

You will always be a piece of the man I continue to become.

CONTENTS

INTRODUCTION

There is a lot of talk these days about "Toxic Masculinity." With that I feel that there is a lot of misunderstanding of the term. I do not use this term at all in the book but felt compelled to address it here. I do not believe that masculinity in and of itself is toxic. There is nothing toxic about having a beer with the boys, scratching your nuts in public, playing sports, being physically strong or sporting a beard. That said, a lot of the societal stereotypes of masculinity that are pushed upon men *are* potentially toxic.

This book is not a "calling out" or even a "calling in." It is a recount of my continual quest to become a better man. It is not prescriptive; it is not all encompassing, and I am certainly no expert. My objective is to spark you to challenge your thinking and perhaps look for new ways to define "success" for yourself. It is my way of sharing my feelings and in turn inspire you to give yourself permission to share yours.

The creation of this book has taken almost 5 years to complete. It encapsulates the incredible journey that has been my life and the lessons I have learned along the way. At times I found myself running with the kind of pack that I now hope to see become completely eradicated: men who subscribed to the negative hyper-masculine tropes that need to become a thing of the past. This book is my effort to assist with that. I hope you will find the stories entertaining and that they will give you pause to reflect on some of the stories in your own life.

All of the events I share are true. In many instances I have changed names to respect the privacy of the individuals involved.

Maybe you'll see some of yourself in my story.

PREFACE:

LESSONS FROM THE BACK OF A POLICE CAR

It is a little after noon on a sunny Friday in Sherwood Park, Alberta, Canada: a suburb of the capital city of Edmonton with a population of about 100,000. Sherwood Park is the seventh largest city in the province but still retains the status of hamlet. What had started out as a fairly routine business meeting over lunch has abruptly come to a halt.

Somehow I now find myself sitting in the back of an unmarked police car in front of the restaurant. Two burly, badass-looking plainclothes officers sit in the front seat, looking back at me over the seat. With the doors locked from the outside, I am trapped to face the unfaceable.

The sights and sounds of the world around me fade into oblivion. The only thing that exists is right here, right now and the impossible message they are delivering.

I cannot fathom what I am hearing. Disbelief courses through every vein, artery, and pore of my being. The mantra running through my mind? *This can't be real. This can't be real. This can't be real. This kind of thing doesn't happen in real life.*

Questions come at me through the fog. I try to comprehend. I want to cooperate, but it doesn't seem to matter.

"Where did you go for dinner? What time did you finish?"

I don't fucking know. Why would I know? Why does that matter? Why does any of this matter at all?

Stop, Mike, don't get angry. Cooperate.

"How can I help? Wait, a receipt. I have a receipt from dinner. Surely the time will be on the receipt."

Am I a suspect? Do they think I had something to do with this?

Holy shit! Of course I am.

I have so many questions. So do they. So, so many questions: "Did you notice somebody following the two of you last night?" "What time did you get to the house?" "Were there any unusual cars parked on the street?"

My head is reeling in disbelief. Suddenly my thoughts jump to the kids.

"What about the kids? Are the kids okay? … What do you mean you can't tell me anything?"

How is this even possible?

They keep on talking but I can't really hear anything. There are two of them, but the one in the passenger seat does most of the talking. I see them watching my reactions.

Do they seriously think I had something to do with this?

Why wouldn't they?

My mind continues to reject what I am hearing, continuing to scream at me: *This can't be real, this can't be real. THIS CAN'T BE REAL!*

They won't tell me anything. Why won't they tell me anything? I don't understand. "Surely you can tell me what has happened."

All they do is ask questions; they never answer them.

"What about the kids? Tell me about the kids, for fuck's sake! Are the kids okay? Where are they right now?"

I try hard not to get angry, to keep my emotions in check, but my resolve is quickly crumbling.

"Wait! What about *my* kids? What else has happened? Is anyone else involved? Should I be worried about their safety? Where are my kids? Is someone protecting them? Are you 'protecting' them from me?!? What. The. Fuck! Why won't you tell me anything?"

I try to keep it together, to stay calm, to not absolutely fall apart. What is the appropriate reaction to this kind of situation? I don't know the answer. There is nothing appropriate about this situation at all.

"Am I being detained? Will I be taken to the station? What the fuck is going on?"

It finally hits me.

This. Is. Real. Very real, and there is absolutely nothing that I can do to change it. There is nothing that can ever prepare you for something like this.

I was certain in the back of that police car that I was in the most challenging time I would ever face. I knew there was nothing in life that could rock my world, challenge my beliefs, or shake me to my core more than the event those two police officers were describing.

I knew beyond a shadow of a doubt in that moment that I was facing the pinnacle of adversity to test my mettle — the single most monumental hurdle in my life.

I was wrong.

In that police car on a Friday afternoon, I had no idea this was only the beginning of a journey that would take me places I never thought possible.

CHAPTER 1

LEAN IN AND FEEL

Think about your last personal crisis. Did you see it also as an opportunity? What if you had? How would that perspective have changed not only how you dealt with it, but maybe more importantly, how you *felt* about it? Were there lessons in that experience? Did you extract them or is that something you have yet to tackle?

We tend to put unrealistic coping expectations on ourselves in times of crisis. It becomes easy to spiral into self-doubt and self-loathing when we do not cope well. We judge our actions and our behaviours, yet we have done little to prepare other than survive for however many years we have been on this planet.

As a long-distance runner, I like to think of the analogy of a marathon. I certainly wouldn't expect someone to go from couch to marathon without running a 5km somewhere in the middle. Or, if I think in terms of children learning to read, I would not hand them *War and Peace* with the expectation that they can muddle their way through from start to finish. Instead, my kids and I started with simple three-letter words, slowly building into sentences, then larger words, and eventually graduating to entire books.

We need to learn patience and self-compassion when it comes to how we deal with crisis. We need to set ourselves up actively for success in the event of a crisis.

That crisp October day in the back of that police car, I had come to a crossroads in my life. I had been presented with circumstances more horrific than I could have ever imagined. Still, I had choices. What was important was that I remained conscious through my experience. What was important was that I chose my own path and had the courage to follow it.

It was about being strong enough to feel all of it — the fear, the disbelief, the doubt, the pain — and keep going.

I may not have had any option about what happened. The only option I had was how I responded to those events. On this occasion, I was being given an opportunity to both measure my progress and practice my response. While this tragedy was not an opportunity I might have wished for — and not even one I would wish upon my worst enemy — I knew that I needed to open myself to the possibility that these events had transpired in order to teach me.

The larger the crisis, the more monumental the event, the more difficult it is to see it from this perspective. At the time, when I got caught in crisis, I went into survival mode. I forgot that the fundamental principles and tools I should have been using are the same no matter the magnitude of the calamity. This is exactly why my regular practice with smaller events had helped to prepare me for the larger ones.

I was fortunate.

I had practiced in the calm to prepare for the storm.

If we accept that crisis in life is inevitable, then it makes a lot of sense to practice wherever we can. God knows we are given ample opportunity to practice remaining calm through the course of the daily routine speed bumps that life throws at us. If we start monitoring, then practicing, our responses to something as simple as our impatience at the irritation of rush hour traffic or our children's wilful defiance, or any of the myriad daily annoyances that we all face, we can start building our resiliency.

Like the survivalist hoarding food, water, and weapons for the approaching apocalypse, we, too, can prepare for the worst well before it happens. In part, that's why I wrote this book — to help you start practicing with the small stuff, so that when the big stuff happens, you're ready. It is about practicing the art of emotional reconnection.

I think it's worth a quick discussion of the word "practice." The word itself can be a bit ambiguous, meaning "to rehearse in order to improve an activity"; as a noun it can mean the activity itself. Understand that when I talk about practicing, I am using it as a verb: "to begin habitually applying a tactic or technique."

You can practice avoidance, carefully scripting the mythical perfect life that we all so desperately seek. Yet no matter how skilled you are in the art of avoidance, life is equally adept. Shit happens. Whether you're a meticulous planner or you prefer to fly by the seat of your pants, life does in fact happen with or without our permission. It will match you for every dip, duck, dodge, or dive you take. You can be as agile as Neo in the movie *The Matrix*, but like Agent Smith, life will keep outmanoeuvring you, reminding you that you are, after all, only human. So unless you have a Trinity to intercept with a "dodge this," then you'd best find ways to practice resilience in order to prepare for those moments.

There are pivotal moments in our lives, those seminal junctures that inexorably change the path of the journey we thought we were on. The sooner in life that we can see these moments for the lessons they are, reflect on them, and learn from them, the closer we will come to finding our capital "T" Truth. It is within these moments we find purpose and meaning.

And it's within these moments that we are given opportunities to practice. I am a big proponent of the power of good questions. At the end of each chapter I have included a couple of questions that I have asked myself at various points in my life. My hope is that they will help awaken something within you. That they will help you become more of 'Who' you are supposed to be.

I wrote this book to share with you the practices that have worked for me in becoming a man of whom I am proud and the practices I continue to use to become the man I want to be.

This is the story of a powerful shift in my life: a departure from setting goals in the traditional sense and the adoption of what I feel is a far superior framework. At first glance it may fly in the face of traditional wisdom, but hear me out:

When I am at my best, instead of setting goals, I instead use a three-part framework.

- I set Values.
- I set Intentions.
- And I set Milestones.

VALUES:

Defining and understanding your core values is critical to the process. Our values become our true north. Our guiding light. The piece that we always test against when faced with making a decision. Identifying and subsequently defining our values is a very important first step.

Intentions:

An intention is all about who you want to be at the given moment. Here are a couple of examples of my intentions:

I help people become the best version of themselves

I intend to leave this world a better place for me being in it

I am love

I allow abundance to come into my life

Milestones:

A milestone is defined as "an action or event marking a significant change or stage in development."

Setting milestones as waypoints or measuring sticks throughout our journey allows us to ensure that we stay on course. We can hold these milestones up against our Values and Intentions as a test.

In telling the story of how this approach originated and evolved in my life, I aim to highlight the beliefs that kept me less than the man I wanted to be and the challenges I faced moving beyond my limiting, toxic mindset. These skewed perspectives of success and manhood aren't unique to my life — I know many men battle with them. If you're one of them, I hope you find in this story a roadmap through the doubt, fear, and insecurity we've been taught to hide from others and from ourselves.

But for now, in order for you to understand who I am and who I want to be, I need to go back a bit, back a lot closer to the beginning.

WHEN SOMETHING'S GOTTA CHANGE:

Our perspective on our life changes how we operate and can change how we feel. Do you look at negative events as an opportunity or as a crisis? The beautiful thing is that we get to decide.

What is a specific crisis you have faced in your life?

____

____

____

____

How would it feel if you started looking at that crisis as an opportunity to practice?

____

____

____

____

CHAPTER 2

REBEL WITHOUT A CLUE

To this day I credit everything good that I am to the solid values on which I was raised. I'm not sure I will ever understand where and why I took the left turn I did in my teens. Maybe my quest to become a badass was built into my DNA. Whatever the reason, I was your stereotypical rebel without a clue.

I can honestly say my parents were not to blame. I was raised in a Christian household with traditional family values. My parents always seemed to have it together.

I am the oldest. My brother Darryl is 20 months my junior, and my sister Judi came along some five years later. There was never any question about how much we were loved as children. Even now, as I discuss my childhood with my mom to ensure I present an accurate depiction, she rattles off a few stories that paint the picture fairly well.

"Perhaps you could tell them about the time when you were three years old," Mom suggests. "You were already toilet trained but far too independent and stubborn to stop playing to go inside to use the bathroom. Instead you just filled your pants. I remember threatening you that, if it happened again, you would have to come in and stay in your room.

After a bit of time outside, you came to the back door, pants stinky full, saying, 'I want to go play in my room.' You seldom let me feel as though I had 'gotten through' to you."

As wilful a child as I was, stubborn and set in my ways, there was never any doubt in my mind that I was loved. Dad worked as a teacher, and Mom was a nurse who worked less than she might have to ensure that we were well taken care of.

All the sports we wanted. Church on Sunday. Regular Sunday dinner with the grandparents and cousins. I'm not sure you could have scripted a more idyllic family setting if you had tried.

This upbringing may have set my expectations for my future family unrealistically high. You know the dream: the house with the white picket fence; two kids, a boy and a girl; a beautiful, kind, and loving wife whom I would work hard to take care of. When I was growing up, I always had that picture-perfect view of what a family was. After all, for the most part, I had lived it.

Pea Soup

As far as I knew, there was never any discord between Mom and Dad. I know in this day and age this may be hard to believe, but I honestly never saw anything that would suggest fighting. The odd disagreement, but never what I would consider a fight.

The closest thing I can remember to any kind of family dissent was the infamous Pea Soup Incident of 1979. It tells you a little something about how aligned my mother and father typically were in the way they raised us that this story stuck around for years — odd because it was such a small thing, really.

One particular evening Mom had made pea soup for dinner. We gathered at the kitchen table to eat, little Judi in her high chair. Darryl and I were sitting at the table, wary to try this dinner that was outside the norm of what we usually ate. Mom, as always, insisted that we at least try the new menu item. (If you have children, you know how well they respond to newly-introduced meal options. Especially green ones.)

After our brave first attempts to eat the soup, my brother and I both vehemently refused to try it again. Mom insisted that we needed to at least finish the serving. You can picture the scene: Mom at wit's end raising three kids, busting her tail to make a nice meal, only to be confronted by two ingrates at the dinner table. As a father now, in hindsight, I completely empathize with her frustration.

I can hear Mom in my head now: "Just wait 'til your father gets home."

When Dad, who often worked late, came home that night after we had sat down to eat, Mom promptly enlisted his authoritarian demeanour so that he, too, insisted we eat the pea soup.

This is when things got interesting.

Dad sat down after asserting his will, tasted the soup, and promptly backtracked.

"Boys, you don't have to eat your soup."

That, my friends, was as close to a fight between my mother and father as I ever recall. Don't get me wrong, I'm sure there was discord, but growing up we never saw it.

I was certainly one of the lucky ones in regard to my family setting. There is no question that my parents gave me everything I could possibly need for a healthy and happy life. But this accord set me up for some pretty pie-in-the-sky dreams of my own future domestic bliss. It's amazing how much our childhood and upbringing shape the rest of our lives.

I was fortunate enough to have been raised with an immense amount of emotional support. Even when things went sideways and I made stupid choices, I now realize that those core values and emotional support I always received were what eventually brought me back on track. Those values had been implanted by the environment in which I was raised.

This truth gives me comfort when I see my own children make poor choices. The values their mother and I instilled in them, along with emotional support we continue to provide, will be their true north, pointing them back in the right direction. Ultimately our emotions drive the decisions we make shaping our behaviours, which eventually produce our results.

I am certainly no psychologist, but it fascinates me, as I reflect on these early childhood memories, just how much they shaped my core values. The consensus from the experts is clear: our childhood experiences have a profound effect on our adult selves.

A number of studies look at this correlation. In one 32-year study, researchers found that babies and toddlers raised in emotionally supportive homes for at least the first three and a half years did better as adults in areas of education, social life, and romantic relationships. On the other hand, Dr. Jonice Webb, a psychologist with over 25 years' experience, coined the term Childhood Emotional Neglect or CEN. She states that "Emotional Neglect is, in some ways, the opposite of mistreatment and abuse. Whereas mistreatment and abuse are parental acts, Emotional Neglect is a parent's failure to act. It's a failure to notice, attend to, or respond appropriately to a child's feelings. Because it's an act of omission, it's not visible, noticeable or memorable. Emotional Neglect is the white space in the family picture; the background rather than the foreground. It is insidious and overlooked while it does its silent damage to people's lives." Dr. Webb's work is definitely worth further exploration, if any of this resonates with you.

Individuals whose emotions are not validated as children may grow up to be adults who have difficulty knowing and trusting their own emotions.

Their emotional self has been suppressed and denied, leaving them feeling disconnected and alone. They may feel like a piece of themselves is missing.

If we agree that our experiences shape our relationship with our emotions, then it stands to reason that our childhood experiences, the ones while our minds were still developing, have had a profound impact on how we view the world and ourselves in it. All those family values and all that accord in my childhood home impacted what I think and choose as an adult, right?

Our emotions drive our decisions.

Now think about every single decision that you make as a waypoint in your life. You can see how important they become, each choice making major, minor, or even miniscule adjustments to your life's trajectory. When you compound that process over the decades you've been on this planet, you can see how each decision, no matter how seemingly insignificant, is what has determined the current position in which you now sit. This is the reason why, for decades, I have sought, and continue to seek, emotional mastery.

Where do you fall on this spectrum of emotional support, stability, and security in your own upbringing? Maybe you didn't have the kind of stable home life I did. Maybe you had a stable upbringing but have never really looked closely at how that example set up certain expectations for your own success in life. Consider the important role your childhood experiences have had on the person you have become today.

As my business partner is fond of saying, "The past and the present do not equal the future."

This is the good news, because how we believe and how we act as a result of those beliefs can change. We can change our minds. The scientific term is "neuroplasticity," the brain's ability to adapt throughout life.

I am a huge fan of understanding the science of things, of knowing the why behind the what. As a result, I have studied a fair bit of neurobiology and the impacts of early childhood development, have read stacks of books written on the subject from a variety of different angles. And my take-away is this: while genetics and early childhood experiences may make us predisposed to certain behaviours and beliefs, those actions and attitudes are not predetermined.

While we may be *predisposed,* we are not *predetermined* to act according to any particular behaviour pattern

Let me say that again, because this is a critically important concept: we may be *predisposed,* but we are not predetermined to act according to any particular behaviour pattern.

So many times in life when we make the decision to make a change, we focus on behaviours or actions. While this may seem like a logical place to start, it is often unsustainable. How many times have we started a pattern of behaviour in order to attempt to create a positive outcome in our lives, only to stop that behaviour shortly thereafter, reverting back to our default patterns? The problem is that we will not consistently behave in a manner that is inconsistent with our feelings. In other words, if we try brute force by "willing" the actions to happen, without first changing whatever fundamental emotion is driving the current behaviour patterns, we will be doomed to fail.

The question then becomes, how do we do change those underlying emotions or at least prevent them from hijacking our behaviour? First off, we need to understand primary and secondary emotions. Primary emotions are our initial reaction, that first core emotion. A secondary emotion is usually a feeling that immediately follows the primary, often acting as a defence mechanism. Many times we are only consciously aware of the secondary emotion; for example, of the anger that masks hurt or sadness.

"The past and the present do not equal the future."

According to Dr. Lisa Firestone, a clinical psychologist, our primary emotions may be triggered by current events, but they can be rooted in our past. The challenge is that before we can identify these primary emotions, they often get steam rolled by secondary emotions, leaving us unable to identify what we need in the moment. Our behaviours become reactive to the secondary emotions and can easily have negative consequences.

A perfect example of an underlying emotion that prevents a positive behaviour in my own life is part of the reason why this book has taken so long to make it to your hands. A few years ago, I had a business coach, and we were discussing my passion for public speaking and writing. We talked about some of the things that were holding me back. I shared with him that certainly one of the things that I wrestled with was self-promotion. When we explored a little further, I expressed my concern about being seen as arrogant or egotistical. You see, I had been brought up to learn that with humility comes wisdom. At one point in the conversation, I said to him, "Yeah, I just never want to be seen as 'THAT guy.'"

He paused before responding, and when he did reply, he said something that completely shifted how I thought of the situation, making me re-evaluate how I felt and everything I believed about this scenario.

"Let me get this straight. You're telling me that you are prepared to withhold the gifts that you have to offer the world simply for fear of being seen as egotistical?"

My perception shifted. I realized that my hesitation wasn't so much rooted in my humility but rather in my fear of being seen as egotistical. Without addressing that deep-seated emotion — fear — there was no way for me to move forward. That one emotional roadblock had the ability to prevent me from living my Truth. The solution was quite simple: address the emotion preventing me from achieving my purpose.

Is fear preventing you from sharing your gifts with the world?

The reality, though, is that while the solution may be simple, it is not easy. It takes practice and repetition to move through that fear. One of the tools in my toolkit is to "lean in" to that fear and allow it to express itself. I can do this by amplifying it and looking at what is the worst-case scenario. I imagine my friends and family reading my promotional material, listening to me talk about the work that moves me. I then imagine them talking behind my back in the worst possible way. I exaggerate the outcome to the *n*th degree. Then I look at the worst-case scenario: people who I thought were friends might think less of me because I am passionate about my work. I try and ride that wave of emotion and feel what that worst-case scenario would feel like, realizing that in truth the hurt is not that bad. Once I lean in, that feeling automatically starts to dissipate. Next, I look at the best-case scenario: I can change individuals' lives with my work. Weighing these scenarios allows me to move forward confidently.

Identifying that this particular fear was holding me back was an important revelation for me. Once I became aware of the emotion that was causing my behaviour, or in this case, *lack* of behaviour, I suddenly had choices for how I could respond to those emotions. This brings to mind a quote from Eckart Tolle, a spiritual teacher and the author of *The Power of Now*: "With awareness there comes choice." You will hear me talk a lot about awareness through these chapters.

While I grew up with what most would call a perfect childhood, those early years are worth reflecting on. How did they shape my beliefs and thoughts, even today? Did that set the bar unrealistically high? Did I have expectations that, when left unmet, made me more disappointed than I might have otherwise been?

Considering the illegal turn my life was about to take, I'd say yes.

WHEN SOMETHING'S GOTTA CHANGE:

Fears, doubts, and all of our insecurities can become a massive barrier to living our purpose. For me it took someone outside to point out these self-limiting beliefs and emotions. We have the opportunity to become our own self coach, to find these barriers on our own. Taking some time to reflect on how and why we see the world is a huge first step.

How has your upbringing shaped your relationship with your emotional self?

___

___

___

What are the underlying emotions that are driving your beliefs and behaviours?

___

___

___

___

CHAPTER 3

REBELS, BOOZE AND BOXCARS

I had just come out of 7th grade — by far my last and best year in elementary school. I had the good fortune of being in a class of academically gifted students, led by a teacher who enjoyed challenging us. We were doing complex math problems and English at closer to an 11th grade level. We learned how to do interesting things like measure the height of a tree using trigonometry. It was an amazing experience, and I felt lucky to be challenged and acknowledged for my accomplishments. Grade 7 was the year that our school first brought in a personal computer. I had an affinity for technology very early on. I would often stay late, sometimes until the janitor kicked me out, experimenting with the lone computer.

While Grade 7 was an absolute joy, I can assure you Grade 8 became the exact opposite as I moved into the larger junior high school with teachers who were far less apt to challenge my thinking. When it became clear that I would not be presented with any challenges in my new school regime, my curious mind started to look elsewhere.

One day, I stole a bottle of what I thought was wine from my parents' basement and took it to school with me. Along with my good friend and fellow computer geek Je, I took the bottle and went down to Robert Burnaby Park to have lunch — and a drink. The park, which was about five blocks from the school, was very large: about 50 hectares of green space within the setting of Burnaby, a Vancouver, British Columbia suburb.

The heavily-wooded park afforded lots of opportunities for two young "men" to get sufficiently lost from civilization, where they would be able to take their first sip of alcohol uninterrupted. It was one of those moments of heady anticipation, part of the journey to badassery, savouring the taste of what it would soon feel like to venture into that previously unknown, forbidden arena of "being a man." Our fear of being caught intermingled with the excitement of crossing the threshold between adolescence and adulthood.

The taste of anticipation, however, was far more delicious than our first taste of alcohol. At the first touch of that liquid hitting our as yet underdeveloped palates, we both almost vomited.

"This wine tastes fucking horrible!"

We almost conceded failure on that first attempt at badassery. Fortunately (or unfortunately, if you're not in Grade 8), we ran into one of the older boys who had a bit of a rebel reputation and subsequently asked him to inspect our wine.

After a quick glance, he threw his 80s style mullet back with the grace of David Lee Roth on tour and laughed with derision. "Dude, this isn't wine. It's Lemon Gin. You need to mix that shit up!"

This may have been my first taste of a more adult dose of shame and embarrassment. My first attempt at high school rebellion was certainly not off to a good start.

"Um, OK?" I really didn't know what exactly that meant, but my partner in crime and I decided that the missing ingredient was likely a soft drink of some kind.

Thank God we were the 'gifted' students. Being the resourceful young lads that we were, Je and I quickly hiked back up to the corner store and purchase a two-litre bottle of 7 Up to use as mix. As programmers and wannabe computer geeks, we were thrilled that we had 'debugged' the situation.

At that point the act of drinking did not have a lot to do with the typical motives for drinking. It wasn't about emotional escape; it wasn't even about typical male bravado. We were both pretty much resigned to the fact that we were never going to be the cool kids. What started out as experimentation had turned into a problem to be solved. Bottle of gin in one hand and bottle of 7 Up in the other; I could call this mission a success.

After that, things are a little unclear, as you may well imagine.

Somehow Je and I became separated. In my euphoric fog, I did the only thing I could think to do: I headed back to school. I'm sure it's not a surprise that this turned out to be a really, really, really bad idea. What did I care? I was young and invincible, and I did not have to answer to anyone.

I headed straight into my science class about half an hour later than I should have. I walked into the class; the smell of Bunsen burners in the air, boiling some chemical cocktail in a variety of conical flasks. Students lined their desks, intent on whatever experiment they were literally cooking up at that time. Some broke their concentration as I stumbled into the room.

My science teacher and I had never seen eye to eye. Ms. Science Teacher in her long white lab coat turned to watch me enter, eyes peering over glasses halfway down her nose, with a burning disdain for the tardy teen who dared darken her doorway. She quickly crossed the room to her desk, grabbed a pad of paper, scribbling a note that she handed to me with instructions to head straight to the principal's office.

As if that was going to happen.

I recall crumpling up the slip of paper as best I could in my inebriated state, shoving it in her pocket, and calling her a not-so-flattering name.

Project rebellion was starting to get a little more on target.

I was clearly not a natural born rebel, though, because of what I did next.

I walked into the office, where I ended up seeing the vice principal who handled the disciplinary issues at the school. The VP also happened to be an acquaintance of my father. Did I mention that my dad was a counsellor at a senior high school across town? Yeah. My day was not getting any better.

I still remember to this day at least part of the speech the vice principal gave me. I remember him talking about what had to happen and that it was for my own edification. He talked about the disappointment I would surely cause my parents. Then Mr. Varro asked me something that would stay with me for a lifetime.

"Do you know the difference between 'hurt' and 'harm,' Mike?"

I could not give him a satisfactory answer, so he went on to explain that "harm" was permanent, while "hurt" was only temporary. "What I have to do might 'hurt' you temporarily, but I would never do anything to cause you harm."

This little punk proceeded to receive the first suspension of his rebel years, marking the beginning of a very long journey of rebellion.

In the months following my return to school, I continued to sneak off to the park to have a drink or smoke a joint from time to time, now more of a habit than an experiment. I am not really sure what the appeal was: alcohol clearly made me an idiot, and all pot did was make me sluggish and hungry.

That year someone had the wisdom and foresight to put an arcade in across the street from the school, much to the chagrin of school staff. Certainly not an environment that left a lot of room for positive personal growth, but the arcade was where I would make some fast friendships, the kind of bond that could only be forged between two teenage boys who were both flirting with the same two teenage girls and who quickly recognized the advantages of teaming up instead of competing.

My memory is spotty at best over the course of those formative teen years. I always had the good fortune of having the solid family foundation at home that I could come back to. Not everyone that I hung out with in those years had the same luxury.

I Love You Man

My best friend Rick was one of those less fortunate kids. I never met his parents, only his twin sister. I never went to his house other than the group homes where he lived and where we often hung out together. While I intentionally shucked the comforts of a loving family in my quest for adventure and rebellion, Rick did not have the same choice. I did not really understand it at the time, nor did I question it, but there certainly must have been a reason why he was in group homes and foster care bouncing from home to home. I'm sure I didn't really understand the gravity of his situation. Even now I'm not certain I fully understand what his life must have been like.

The one thing I know for certain is that there was a deep bond between us. Rick was the first man in my life who was not a relative to whom I ever said "I love you." I don't recall where Rick and I met, but I do have a recollection of being reunited at Marlborough re-entry school, a program designed for kids who had either flunked out or been kicked out of school. Rick and I both fit that second criteria. The noble intention, I suspect, was to get kids back up to speed and reintegrated into the regular school system. It doesn't take a rocket scientist to spot the obvious problem: you ended up with all the bad apples in the same barrel. I can't imagine what it would have been like as a teacher in that environment, and honestly, I don't recall even attending those classes, although I must have. What I do remember is that Marlborough was where things really started to go sideways for me.

Rick and I had a great time. We found ways to kill our day in the most unproductive manner possible. There were days where we would catch a bus or walk down to New Westminster, the next suburb to the south. We would hang out by the railway tracks along the Fraser River. We would sit in the brush smoking cigarettes or joints depending on the economics of the moment. We'd bullshit, throw rocks, talk about the injustice of a system that expected us to go to school. Sometimes we'd watch as a train headed our direction over the bridge in the distance, listening to the whistle blow as it slowed to cross the river. Wheels squealing on steel, audible for miles. The clickety clack as the train meandered across the river and made the sharp turn to follow the bank north. The smell of the diesel engines getting closer and closer.

We'd watch and smoke, and watch and smoke, sometimes catching the eye of a conductor. It was mesmerizing, taking us mentally far away from the reality of everyday life.

At some point we must have noted that the train slowed down substantially coming off the bridge. I'm not certain who came up with the idea first, but if you close your eyes and put yourself in the minds of two 13-year-old boys, you can hear the macho male challenge: "We should hop it!"

What started as a joke morphed into a dare. That dare very quickly became a plan. We started to look for an empty boxcar with the doors open, always keeping an eye out for a railway employee before making our move. We scouted several trains over several different days before mustering the courage to actually make our move. It was easy to find reasons why each car wasn't appropriate to hop.

"I think I saw a railway security guard."

"That one's not slowing down."

"The doors are closed on that one."

Eventually the time came where we had to just suck it up and go. I suspect that, on that day we finally found the perfect train — coming off the bridge at the perfect speed, with no security in sight and a boxcar door open – Rick was the one to make the first move. He was definitely the more daring of the two of us. Once he put his skinny little ass in high gear pacing the train, I knew I had no choice but to join him.

Legs pumping, heart racing, palms sweating, we ran alongside that locomotive with everything we had, our eyes vacillating between the boxcar and the uneven footing we were running on, careful not to miss a step or trip on a railway tie. An errant step could result in a face plant under the moving train that we might not recover from. The sounds, the smells, the exhilaration! That natural high of adrenaline surpassed the satisfaction of any of the chemical substances we had ever used. Rick ran, he jumped; I followed his lead as he reached out a hand to help pull me up, and just like that we were safely inside a moving boxcar.

"Yeehaaaaw!"

"Fuck, yeah! That was something else!"

We had no idea where we were going but anticipated that we would end up at the train yards over in North Vancouver, which is exactly what happened. Coming from New Westminster, we meandered through Coquitlam, Port Coquitlam, Port Moody, along the waterfront, eventually having to cross Burrard Inlet. We entered a tunnel that was as black as the midnight sky on a moonless night. No light, just noise and fumes and an eerie sense of solitude. To add to the surreal feeling of flying across a railroad track in pitch black, we came shooting out of the tunnel directly onto the bridge across the inlet. Crossing a bridge while riding in an open boxcar on a freight train is a terrifying experience, though I'm certain neither of us would have admitted that at the time.

Once we had made the trip the first time, it became a bit of a "thing to do" from then on. Although we had a few run-ins with railway security once the train stopped in the yard, we were faster than any of the security we met and never got caught. We became something akin to experts in the art of train hopping, learning the schedules and which trains went where on which days. It made for a remarkable way to kill a day.

As I write this — now a father to two teenagers myself — all I can think is, "Holy shit, you were a complete idiot." Yes, I could have easily been one of those news stories of a crushed body on the tracks, losing a limb or worse.

I could write reams of stories about my pursuit of manhood, from smoking joints on school field trips to dropping acid with Rick. Soon, my pursuit of badassery included a list of petty criminal offenses that I was fortunate were never discovered. It was only dumb luck that prevented me from dying or being thrown in jail.

I can assure you that by the time I hit my mid teens, my parents were at their wits' end. At some point, I was just beyond reach for them. They simply did not know what to do with their rebellious little teenager — the one who believed he had learned all that life had to teach at the ripe old age of 16.

Some of us take much too long to grow out of that teenage

cockiness.

Sometimes I think we all have the ability to revert to a teenage mentality. We hold the power now that we lacked in our youth — be it money, strength, or influence. I know I fight this temptation hard when dealing with my children when they're rebelling against my authority. In these moments, I try and step back, take a breath, and remember what I was like when I was a teen searching for empathy.

Immediately following that exercise, I remind myself that I am no longer 16. But I have to wonder if there are still times when I act like that. Train hopping might have been replaced with ice climbing, rock climbing, ultra marathons and long-distance triathlons. Though perhaps different in stupidity levels, they are eerily similar in potential outcomes and adrenaline rushes. The difference being that as an adult I was taught, trained, and practiced for all of those activities. Challenging the boundaries, pushing the limits, and seeking to prove something to myself — I am ok with that as long as I am indeed trying to prove something to myself and not anyone else.

I believe that success comes when you stop trying to prove to the world how good you are and start trying to prove to yourself how much better you can be.

I think sometimes my inner teen still pushes hard, scratching at the surface of my being, longing to escape and express himself.

Over lunch recently I listened to my friend Bonnie lament the challenges she is having with her teenage son. He is starting to test the waters of rebellion, testing boundaries and blazing his own trail. While Bonnie was out one night, her son and his friends took advantage of the empty house to party — much to the chagrin of her short-tempered neighbour. The neighbour confronted the boys, challenging them on their manhood, and in typical mob mentality, the boys were emboldened by numbers and youthful bravado. As the scene escalated, the neighbour went back inside and brought out his dog, threatening to sic him on the boys if they didn't disperse. Eventually the neighbour chased them into the house, called the police, and the entire event was brought to an abrupt conclusion. A home security camera caught the taunting and escalation on the part of the neighbour.

I'm not suggesting that a teenage son bringing friends back to an empty house was acceptable, but is that how a mature adult handles a tough situation with kids? What would have happened if the dog had injured one of the boys? What if tensions had escalated to a point of violence? Was it some deep-seated insecurity that brought up a need for the neighbour to outdo these teenage boys? Did his inner teen break through the surface? Did he lack the emotional intelligence to be aware of his anger and manage it appropriately?

Hurt is temporary, harm is permanent.

Mr. Varro's lesson would serve me well later in life, much more than I might have suspected. As a business leader and later a father, this mantra rings in my ears anytime I have to make a decision on how to deal with a situation that requires disciplinary action of some kind. Perhaps the lesson here is to channel that inner teen and ensure that he isn't actually manifesting negatively in some way in our current life. It is easy to let our emotions get the best of us in tense situations. What matters is how we deal with these times. We need to come up with a plan ahead of time to ensure we have a strategy to deal with the challenges that life throws at us.

One of my favourite strategies to deal with heat-of-the-moment situations where I am called upon to make a decision, especially if I realize my emotions may get in the way, is to ask myself a simple question: "What would the person I *want* to be do in this circumstance?" I first heard this from my friend and leadership expert Drew Dudley. It is amazing how easy the decision becomes when I put it into that context.

While controlled, purposeful rebellion is the catalyst to all massive change, it's important to recognize that we can all be caught releasing our inner 16-year-old in ways that are not really befitting the person we want to be.

Usually, when I reflect on where I came from and the behaviours I demonstrated as an angst-ridden teen, it gives me a great appreciation for the beautiful young human beings I have the privilege of raising. As often as I may get frustrated by some of their teenage choices, very little they do puts them even close to the stupidity through which I put myself and my parents at their ages.

Because as you will soon learn, train jumping was not the stupidest or riskiest thing I did in those years.

WHEN SOMETHING'S GOTTA CHANGE:

While we may physically grow out of our teens, it is easy to hang on to some of that youthful rebellion. When harnessed properly our inner rebel can be a great thing. When left unchecked it can be disastrous.

What are the current equivalents of dope smoking and train hopping in your life?

____

____

____

____

How can you best channel your inner rebel in a manner that befits the person you want to be and create the mark you want to leave on the world?

____

____

____

CHAPTER 4

INTO THE NUMB

While train hopping was likely the most dangerous physical activity in which I took part during high school, it definitely was not the riskiest.

I loathe writing these next words, knowing that my beautiful, angelic children will be reading them someday and hoping they will never disappoint my higher expectations for them. But it would not be fair to paint a portrait of youthful me who did not continue to engage in stupidity along the way.

Between ages 13 and 18, I experimented with a variety of chemical substances. I followed the lead of many other misguided youths seeking refuge and meaning — or perhaps just a release from emotions I did not understand — in some of the mind-altering chemicals readily available. The most accessible from a budgetary standpoint were those that could be found naturally: psilocybin or "shrooms," a.k.a. magic mushrooms, a hallucinogen, producing an altered state of consciousness similar to that of the synthetic drug LSD. Of course, at 15 or 16 years old, I didn't really care about synthetic vs. natural. They were free — and that was good enough for me.

My friends and I ran around town looking for green spaces where mushrooms would be growing. No, we weren't getting our shrooms from any sort of reliable source. We apparently felt qualified to determine which mushrooms we happened to find growing in the park were of the "get high" nature vs. the "I'm gonna kill you dead" variety. In a time well before the internet, we had to rely on knowledge passed down from stoner to stoner on what the *good* mushrooms were. It must have been quite the sight for anyone who saw us: a couple of teenage head-bangers with hair halfway down our backs, carefully examining the grassy area of a public park as if one of us had dropped our car keys.

Lucy In The Sky

It's pure luck that neither I nor my friends ingested anything lethal. Sometimes we would choke down the fungus with some type of alcoholic beverage, but when we had access to a house with a kettle, we preferred to boil them into tea. The first time we scraped together a few dollars to obtain the much more powerful hallucinogen LSD, or acid, it scared the shit out of me. I had made my way down to New Westminster where Rick lived in a group home. Without cell phones, smart phones, pagers or the like, I have no idea how we ever found each other in those days. Anytime we were together, we did stupid stuff like knock over mailboxes and test car doors looking for ones that were unlocked so we could loot them for spare change.

In any event, Rick happened to be dealing acid at the time and had a sheet of "White Lightning." I took a hit with Rick, who was already high, and we wandered around for about an hour on a dark evening with no point, purpose, or reason for being.

Shortly after the acid kicked in that night, Rick looked at me and said, "I'm done, I'm heading home."

Now, you should know that LSD is not a drug that you go to sleep on, so you can imagine my strung-out bewilderment at his statement. When I questioned him, he went on to explain that he had dropped his acid around midday, so he was just coming down some 12 hours later. At the time, I'm sure it made sense to me. Still, I had just dropped my first hit of acid and was about to be left alone for the night to wrestle with an 8 to 12-hour high all by myself.

I had no idea what to do, so I started walking home. By now it was the middle of the night. My parents would be asleep, and I thought I could safely sneak in and ride out the high in my bedroom. As I wandered home, I cycled between a narcotic-induced euphoria and a hallucination-induced terror. I could see the streets crack open and blood start to bubble up. I would pause to get my bearings, only to find my arms, legs, and torso covered with a million tiny, green worms. (While it's been over 35 years since that night, the memory of those aberrations in consciousness is etched firmly in my mind.)

I finally made it home, too scared to go upstairs to my bedroom lest my parents greet me. I ended up hiding in the downstairs bathroom, completely terrified at what was happening to my mind and my body yet determined to ride it out.

As I sat on the toilet willing the sensations to pass, they only got worse. Every time I touched my skin, it felt like my fingers sank into melted flesh, similar to the scene in *Raiders of the Lost Ark* where the ark of the covenant is opened and spontaneously melts everyone's flesh. My tongue felt like a swollen mass inside my mouth, threatening to push through the skin of my cheeks at any moment. I tried to shift my focus and concentrate on my surroundings, only to have the walls begin to bubble and boil. I was extremely close to waking my parents up and admitting what I had done so that I could get some help. But I decided I could handle it alone.

I eventually fell asleep.

I wish I could tell you that I thought, "I'm never going to fucking do that again!" After sharing my experience with my stoner buddies, we concluded that the problem wasn't in taking the acid. The problem was in taking the acid and being left alone outside of a "safe" environment.

"Dude! What the fuck were you thinking? You never drop Cid alone! Next time make sure you're not alone, you've got some good tunes and a few joints to take the edge off. Let me know when you want to go again. I just got a great batch of Purple Microdot."

I just had to ensure that any subsequent usage was done in the safety of a basement with music, dim lights, and a little marijuana to ensure a good trip. I told you I was a bit of a problem solver.

This turned out to be an accurate assessment. My subsequent experiences were never quite as bad as that first time. White Lightning lead to Purple Microdot and then to Blue Blotter. LSD never did become a favourite, nor did it become a drug I actively sought out, but I certainly did not shy away from future use.

While marijuana was really the drug of choice for our little gang, we also experimented with opiates like cocaine. We started with a cocaine-laced joint that produced an incredibly satisfying high. From there, my reasoning at that level of maturity was, if a laced high was good, then certainly a snorted high must be much better. Fortunately, even I drew the line at injections. I think I equated injected drugs with addiction and homelessness, so it wasn't something I was ever willing to try.

I used drugs to escape uncomfortable feelings as a kid

Truth be told, it was more likely that I lacked the intestinal fortitude to stick a needle in my arm. Thank God for that small mercy.

As much as I dislike acknowledging this part of my youth, if I don't face it, I don't learn from it. Sadly, I used drugs to escape uncomfortable feelings as a kid. Although I don't know that I could have articulated my emotions at that time, I found it easier to suppress them with drugs and rebellion than to actually explore or attempt to talk about them. Was it simply a mask for feelings that I believed would not serve me? Could it have been a fear of not meeting societal expectations?

I was a teenager looking to make his mark in this world, looking for my area to stand out. It was clear to me early on that I thought differently than a lot of the other kids. I would never be one of the cool kids. I would never stand out as the athlete or the good-looking one. I suppose I had options at how I could stand above the crowd, so to speak. It was always in me to seek out that unique place in the world. I undoubtedly had the mental capacity to go another direction. I could have thrown myself into studies and excelled as I had done in my early school years. I could have followed my curiosity in computer sciences and likely been one of the best "nerds" around. Sadly, at that point in my life I lacked the awareness of the opportunities around me.

We suppress and avoid to block out the pain or discomfort.

Even all these years later, I still see in myself, my peers, friendship circles, and colleagues, that desperation to "fit in" with the cool kids. We want to be in that clique with the people who are, by definition, the minority. There are more of us than there are of them, yet we strive for acceptance into that small group.

If we spent more time as the majority looking for ways to prop each other up, rather than trying to join a clique in which we don't belong, we would not have the same challenges with things like loneliness and depression that we do today.

While as a teen I turned to drugs and rebellion to numb myself to the possibility of feeling, I see such decisions continue into adulthood in a variety of ways. Even if you have never experienced this kind of drugged quest, you likely have had a foolish period of your life that looks a lot like a mistake and was at its core driven by your desire to be more than you *felt* you were. For adults, these desires can still manifest as things as blunt and obvious as drug or alcohol abuse, gambling, or other addictions. There are more insidious ways we drive ourselves into the numb that we do not acknowledge. Addictions and the like, while incredibly difficult to deal with, are far easier to identify than many of the more subtle forms of numbing that I would call "emotional avoidance."

Emotional avoidance is the largest barrier to personal growth and living your true, authentic self. Fighting our emotions is like trying to swim upriver. If we struggle and try and swim against the current, we will become exhausted and eventually become overwhelmed and drown. If we turn our focus to riding downstream, we can ride out the current, sooner or later making our way to the safety of the shore. We cannot selectively numb emotions. When we numb the negative emotions, we also numb the positive ones. We need to stop labelling emotions as "good" or "bad" and learn that all of them shape who we are. We need to learn to lean into them: observe them, sit with them, and learn from them what we can.

It is incredibly important to be hyper-vigilant in monitoring our use of avoidance techniques, mundane or everyday distractions we may not even know we are employing — social media, eating, exercising, workaholism, housework, television — many of which are even recognized societally as virtues. As children we often did not have the wherewithal to speak up, defend, or acknowledge the stress we were feeling. The result is that we did the only things we *could* do. We suppressed and avoided to block out the pain or discomfort.

While these tactics may work well in the short term, they become problematic for the long term. We address the symptoms rather than considering the root causes of how we feel. I could just as easily take up working too much as gambling or any other long list of bad habits to do the same thing as an adult. But as adults, we have the option to look back and learn from our youth, making active choices to repeat or not repeat the mistakes we made back then.

When I discussed my teenage years recently with my mom, she listed the many approaches she and Dad had attempted in their efforts to rein me in: tough love, accountability, freedom, freedom with repercussions, all tempered with their unconditional love and belief that God loved me and protected me, no matter my behaviour. She recounted a time where they had found what they assumed were stolen goods in my bedroom and reported me to the police. Nothing came of that reporting. On another occasion they received a call from the police that I had been picked up for a charge of drunk and disorderly. They agreed to let me spend the night in the drunk tank and have Dad pick me up the next morning. The more boundaries they gave me, the more I rebelled. When I would come home after curfew, they would leave a sleeping bag in the garage for me and lock the door.

For me it was all about adding to my "badass" résumé, and regardless of consequences my behaviour did not change. I remember desperately wanting to have my parents kick me out of the house so that I could be part of *that* tribe. I pushed as many buttons as I could, to no avail. Mom and Dad did their best to accommodate me without disrupting the rest of the family.

The most difficult time for Mom and Dad was when I "seriously ran away from home" somewhere around Grade 10. For about two weeks they had no idea where I was living. Eventually they found out that I had been with some guy from New Westminster. I have a very vague recollection of this period and do not even recall where I met this man, though I am sure I concocted some story of teenage tragedy that convinced him to allow me to stay with him. His condition was always that I had to stay in school. As you can imagine, that did not last very long.

After about two months or so Mom and Dad came home from a weekend away and found me sitting in the family room. "I'm home," I said, with zero explanation. At that time, they told me I could stay on the condition that we went for family counselling. I grudgingly attended the first appointment with the counsellor a few weeks later, but on leaving announced that if they needed counselling, they should go for it, but I didn't and would not go for another appointment. So that was the end of counselling.

I remember one incident of which I'm particularly ashamed. I had been forbidden to go out but had left the house anyhow. I had gone with Rick, and Dad followed us down the street in his car. He eventually got out to confront me and get me back home. Rick intervened and short of Dad using physical force, I wasn't going anywhere. I remember Dad shaking in frustration, clearly at his wits' end. I remember Rick and I laughed as he eventually gave up the fight and got back into his car driving home.

They had moved me to three different schools in the hopes that I would respond to a new environment. They engaged the youth leaders at the church that I had grown up with to try and model for me a better way. And they had enlisted the power of the Lord to the best of their ability by praying and by having the entire congregation pray for me.

I'm sure it won't shock you to learn that, because of the way I was going, I never did see the joys of senior high school, which in Canada is Grades 11 and 12. I dropped out of school somewhere mid-Grade 10, interesting to me now that I have a son and daughter who have made it farther in school than I did. As a father of teenagers, I often reflect on how I would handle similar situations if my children behaved as I did for my parents.

Fortunately for my beleaguered parents, there was an authority figure they thought I might respond to, and they finally sent me far, far away from the trouble I was in.

WHEN SOMETHING'S GOTTA CHANGE:

Actively looking at the patterns we have used in the past and the ones we use now is an excellent exercise to ensure we are still moving in the right direction. Scheduling this on a regular basis is a critical path to finding your purpose.

What habits did you use as a kid to avoid or deal with your feelings?

____

____

____

____

What habits are you using today that [still] interfere with your ability to cope with your emotions?

____

____

____

CHAPTER 5

UNCLE JOHN

My mother Marianne and her four siblings were born in Taiwan while their parents served as Christian missionaries there. My mom's brother John — Uncle Johnny to me — was a bit of a black sheep rebel himself. In 1962 he left Hong Kong on a cruise ship bound for Sydney, Australia as a stowaway. Some guys he met at a bar hid him on the ship on which they worked.

You see, John had wrecked an employer's car earlier and decided the cruise ship was a better alternative than staying in Hong Kong to face the music. The long and short of John's journey was that, once he reached Australia, he busted his ass to make a life for himself, starting on a fishing boat, and eventually becoming a major partner in Marconsol fisheries, a multi-million dollar, publicly traded company. Now he was married and successful with four kids of his own.

So when Mom and Dad sat me down and said, "How'd you like to go live with Uncle Johnny in Australia?" I was over the moon.

While my parents were hoping for some serious life lessons, in my 16-year-old know-it-all mind, I was being given the opportunity to head to the Land Down Under and hang out with a folk hero in my family. John epitomized what I wanted for my life: rebel done good. And a millionaire! He lived by the Golden Rule. No, it's not likely the Golden Rule you're thinking. Uncle John's Golden Rule was simple: The man with the gold makes the rules.

So that was it. That was the solution to the three-year problem of "what the heck you do with a teenage son run amok." You ship him off to a penal colony.

I still have a beat-up old picture of me in all my teenage wannabe glory that day in 1985 at the Vancouver International Airport as I departed for the 18-hour flight, sporting my Stormrider jean jacket and hair halfway down my back like Bruce Dickinson, lead singer from Iron Maiden, and with my small, frail Grandma Cameron standing beside me.

Once I landed in Australia, I had to clear customs. That's when I remembered I had a 4-inch metal hash pipe in the chest pocket of my Stormrider, a memento that Rick had given me before I left Canada. I have no idea how that made it through security in the first place, but it did. As you can imagine, at this point I was starting to sweat: a timid 16-year-old who looked like he had just crawled out of a Cheech and Chong movie trying to find a way to explain away this drug paraphernalia. Thoughts of cavity searches by aggressive Aussie customs agents started swirling through my mind. I didn't have any drugs on me but realized that was going to be a tough sell to Australian immigration authorities who had just pulled a very well-used hash pipe from my pocket.

My Uncle John was waiting on the other side of customs for me and by this time was likely wondering where the hell I was. I had alternating visions of a 250-pound customs officer snapping on his latex gloves to do a complete cavity search and of the fury of my Australian guardian for my idiotic mistake.

I was scared shitless.

Fortunately for me, none of the scenarios I had in mind played out at all. After the officer unwrapped all of the family Christmas gifts I had been tasked to deliver and searched through all of my luggage to ensure I did not have any drugs, he handed me back the hash pipe and said, “You might want to clean it out before you head home.”

I was stunned. I quickly moved from stunned to terrified again, knowing Uncle John would be waiting. I walked into the arrivals area after coming out of customs, some 30-45 minutes after the rest of the passengers. My mind raced to come up with some plausible story as to why I was so late getting through customs. To my relief, Uncle John simply hugged me and said something to the effect of, “Last one off the plane, were you?” I nodded in quiet agreement and off we went to his house.

Uncle John and Aunt Carly lived just outside of Cairns, Queensland in a beautiful large bungalow on the top of a hill with a stunning 360-degree view of the surrounding area. This was definitely the life. I was excited to be somewhere beautiful and warm, and I felt like an adult in control of my own destiny. Now that I had moved across the world away from the “tyranny and oppression” of my parents, life was bound to be perfect.

Looking back, I am not really certain how I thought changing my geography would do anything to address the feelings that were causing me turmoil. The phrase “You can run but you can’t hide” comes to mind.

Uncle John and Aunt Carly made me feel right at home. Carly was the mother of John’s oldest children and both his first wife and his third, the two of them together again after a hiatus in which John married another woman and had two more children.

That first full day in Australia, Carly and the cousins took me snorkelling and we enjoyed some of the best that nature has to offer when it comes to marine life. I went back home with a ridiculous sunburn. (So much for coming from a Canadian winter and diving right into the deep end.) But that was the extent of my tourist days, because at that same time, the boats had come back from being out to sea fishing for prawns. There was work to do, and I had not been sent to Australia for a holiday. I was there to work and presumably "turn my life around."

Uncle John's fishing company owned a fleet of 100-foot prawn trawlers that spent weeks out at sea. That first day on the dock was an eye-opener for sure. The sound of sailors yelling and cursing, the seagulls hovering overhead looking for scraps, and the smell of sweet sea air mixed with the vile stench of diesel fumes set the scene for my next several months of life. When the boats were out to sea, they would snap freeze anything they caught and store them in 50-pound boxes in the boat's deep freeze. By the time the boats came in, there were hundreds of boxes of prawns that had to be unloaded. I was sent to work to assist unloading the boats. When I arrived at the dock and was identified as a "Canuck," I was immediately sent down into the freezer to toss boxes up, since, clearly, being from Canada made me an expert in all things cold.

I was not a strong young man — and I probably weighed 119 pounds soaking wet — but tossing 50-pound boxes with the rhythm of lift, pivot, throw, pivot, lift, pivot, throw, pivot became my norm for the next ten hours. I can assure you that every ounce of muscle fibre felt it the next day. My arms and back were stiff and sore from a workout like no other I had ever experienced. Somehow, though, I was determined to make my mark and not let my uncle down. And there was no way in hell that I was going to let this job kick my ass.

After work, we ended up at the local pub at what was dubbed

a "skippers meeting." Now, whether or not they actually did any business or not, I have no idea. I do, however, recall a lot of alcohol and a lot of loud, boisterous men who were, frankly, intimidating as hell. As the evening wore on and the cacophony grew, I became more and more intrigued with this new lifestyle that I had previously only imagined possible in storybooks and pirate movies. Of course, what resonated with me most was that no one seemed to acknowledge the fact that I was 16 in a bar where the legal drinking age was 18. The men treated me like one of their own, either as a rite of passage or some kind of hilarious joke. For all I knew, they had bets on who could get the young Canuck sick or push him to quit first. In any event, a part of me felt like I was home. It was a welcome change to the culture in Canada where it felt like someone my age was simply a teenager with no apparent value in society — and certainly no adult rights or privileges.

I heard many stories of the abuse of young deckhands by the older more seasoned crew, including beatings in the event of a mistake. The chances of my making a mistake as a 16-year-old weakling who had never sailed before were extremely high. Couple this with the fact that I was the owner's nephew, and I was not likely to get a lot of leeway from the crew.

There was a particular skipper named Mick with whom I got along well, and having him on my side was about the only hope I had of surviving a voyage out into the open seas in search of prawns. Fortunately for me, the voyages weren't as harrowing as I anticipated. Mick was a strong advocate and teacher. I worked my ass off, but I kept my head down and survived.

I think my son Chris was about 14 when I eventually told him this story. I tried to do it somewhat casually, not making a big deal out of it, but he is a bright boy.

"What!? Wait a minute. Wait a minute! So you're telling me that you were so bad that Grandma and Grandpa had to ship you off to

Australia?" When I conceded this was true, his face broke out in a wide grin. "Isn't that where they used to send criminals?"

And there it was, my youthful indiscretions being filed away for a day when he might need to bring them up.

My youthful rebellion, and how I felt at that time, is something I try and keep in mind as I raise my teenagers. It is easy to dismiss our children's wants and needs for seemingly practical reasons, forgetting that they are human beings, too. Our kids have the same desires as any of us: to feel valued, respected, and worthy. My rebellion was a symptom of my troubles, not the cause of them. This is an important point of which to take note: we too often treat the symptoms rather than trying to address the root cause. This was maybe my first lesson in this concept, but it certainly wasn't my last.

We too often treat the symptoms rather than trying to find the root cause.

Surprisingly, working for Uncle John was the first successful remedy for my rebellion. If you're able to find a way to give rebels what they want, at least in some measure, they soon find there is actually nothing against which to rebel. Certainly, the environment I was in was not handcrafted for impressionable young teenagers but somehow worked to quell some of my rebellious urges.

Here, it seemed, what mattered was effort: something I had in spades. Never one to shy away from a challenge or hard work, I relished the opportunity to prove my worth and value to these men. I had to keep it together in a way I hadn't been forced to back home. Okay, I had messed up in school and my parents were upset with me. I had become so hardened that there was no amount of logic or reason that my parents could have bestowed upon me that would have gotten through. By giving me permission to work hard and play hard, Uncle Johnny did start to make a difference in my attitude.

Even today, when I throw myself completely into work I'm

passionate about and then throw caution to the wind when I let off steam afterward, I feel a kind of satisfaction I find hard to describe, as if my restless soul is still for a brief moment. Knowing what quells the rebel within you is essential if you're going to live as a committed, responsible human being.

At that age, having an authority figure I respected hand me a beer after a long day of hard manual labour made an impact on me. It was the only way I was going to become open to learning the lessons that I needed to learn. I was taught that hard work was rewarded: a lesson that I had heard in the past, and certainly one that I would have to receive again in the future before it would truly sink in. I lived up to my end of the bargain and worked hard. In return I was rewarded for that. It was a valuable lesson.

This part of my journey was another chink in the armour, another softening of that hard exterior wall that I had put up in rebelling against my parents. In martial arts training, they talk about force being met with redirection, not resistance. My anger was being redirected. I was not forced to go on the defensive; Uncle John met me where I was. It was a subtle, yet powerful shift in approach. I am extremely grateful that the adults in my life had the wisdom to see the value in shifting methodology.

Back in Australia, at that moment in time, my life was spectacular — hard labour and all. At that age, without a care in the world, with good beer, good times, good family, and good friends, I had my whole life ahead of me.

Until I didn't.

WHEN SOMETHING'S GOTTA CHANGE:

Uncle John was a mentor, a role model who came into my life at the right time and had a significant impact on me. My experience with him would alter the trajectory of my life.

Who are some of the mentors in your life and how have they shaped who you have become?

____

____

____

____

Where can you find opportunity to mentor someone else and what impact might you have on them?

____

____

____

____

CHAPTER 6

GRATITUDE

I had many epic adventures while I lived Down Under, some of my most incredible life experiences up to that time, in fact. From concerts to motorcycles, girls to beer and pot, without question, Australia made an impression on me. Although despite my parents' hopes for my time there, the problems themselves did not magically go away.

My oldest cousin Chris was definitely the rebel of the family. At 19, he had access to the kind of things I cared about at that time: booze, drugs, and music. As you might well expect, Chris and I hit it off immediately. He enjoyed smoking dope; so did I. He enjoyed playing and listening to rock music, as did I. And he definitely shared my affinity for alcohol. He became the big brother I never had.

Much to the chagrin of my uncle, Chris took me under his wing and let me into his circle of friends. We attended an exceptional Dire Straits concert. We didn't exactly buy tickets to the concert; Chris's friend Conrad had a motorhome that we parked outside the wall of the outdoor stadium. We then sat on the roof and drank beer while watching the concert from that nose-bleed vantage point, none of which cost us a dime.

Chris took me on a number of motorcycle rides, my first road bike experiences. I remember loving the feeling — the wind in your face, nothing but air and a whole lot of CCs between you and the road. I will never forget one particular incident where my cousin, presumably trying to show off for a girl, turned and looked over his shoulder and said, "Hold on!" I assumed we were in for a quick acceleration to make a notable exit, so I grabbed the back of the seat behind my bum like I always did. I mean, I wasn't about to wrap my arms around my dude cousin, now was I? Yeah, that was a mistake. Chris had bigger intentions than I anticipated. He popped the clutch, gunned the gas, and pulled the front tire off the ground in a full-on wheelie. My head snapped back and momentum pulled me down, my feet up beside his face, head inches from the pavement, struggling to stay on the bike. He brought it down immediately and we laughed off into the night.

Being 16, I wasn't quite capable of absorbing these not-so-subtle cautions life was throwing at me. I can assure you that by the end of the evening I was off again, smoking a joint or drinking a beer with cousin Chris. A blip on the radar, a lesson received but not one learned.

Then there was the girl, a young lady who was a friend of Chris. Beautiful, fun, and infatuated with this young Canadian who had come to visit. I had had zero experience with women. I think I liked the idea of them simply because they were what young men were supposed to be into. She was intent on making the connection and pursued me. I did what I knew to do, which was not much at all. If memory serves, we got to a point of stripping down to underwear when things went a little sideways for a young boy who had far more testosterone than he knew what to do with. Let's just say that encounter was a little premature. The best part of this story is that a few years later, I took some major ribbing from my cousins who knew how smitten she was in spite of my indifference. The reason for the ribbing? She went on to become some kind of international supermodel.

I learned to drive over there, ultimately getting my learner's license behind the wheel of Chris's Holden Torana (say it with an Aussie accent). Although I turned 17, I was still legally too young to get in the bar, but I was a resourceful young lad. Back then, drivers' licenses didn't have pictures on them, only height, weight, and eye colour. Fortunately, Chris's friend Glen Lewis Chapman and I shared those attributes, except that "Chappy" was old enough to get into the bars. All I needed to do was memorize the other details on the license — Glen Lewis Chapman, 5' 8", 155 pounds, born the first of June and in 1966 — so that when quizzed by the doorman, I could rattle off the specs as if they were my own. It's funny how I remember those details to this very day. I guess you could say this was my first foray into sales.

Life was good... or so I thought, until one day in March when I woke up bleary-eyed, confused, angry, and with a tube in my chest, a pipe down my throat, and no way to communicate at all.

Life was good until I woke up nearly dead.

It was March of 1986, and to be honest, I can't really tell you what happened firsthand. I've pieced the evening together from other people's accounts and some assumptions after the fact. The thing I find oddest about the story is that it took place after we left a Chinese food restaurant. At 17, I had absolutely no taste for (a more apt description would be a disdain for) Chinese food. How is it possible, then, that such a life-changing experience happened on the way home from a night of Chinese food? It still makes no sense at all to me. It's funny the little details we get hung up on.

To this day I have no recollection of the accident, the dinner preceding it, or even leaving the house to go out. But here's what

I've put together: my new buddy Max (a friend of my cousin), his girlfriend, and I were riding together in Max's vehicle. Knowing Max, he had some Judas Priest or Scorpions blaring on the stereo, and we were having a blast. Living the teenage dream, as it were. Max drove from the right front seat, as is done in the land of Aus, and his girlfriend sat in the passenger seat. An eager young Canadian sat in the middle back seat, leaning between the front bucket seats to be part of the action. I picture the Judas Priest song "Living After Midnight" playing at full blast, or perhaps "Breaking the Law" would be more apropos, since it's safe to assume we were, in fact, breaking the law and driving much faster than we should have been. The beat thumping, wheels blurring, me wailing and bouncing to the music in the back seat as the skies opened up in the summer heat of the Australian rainy season. When the rains came, they came hard.

Road slick with fresh rain, car fast, music loud, and the laws of physics waiting to wreak havoc on an otherwise gorgeous evening. The curvature of the road on the familiar route home, the wet pavement, and the tires simply letting go of their grip. Sliding fast, out of control. The raucous, joy-filled expressions of carefree youths quickly replaced with abject terror as the car careened sideways into the corner. A quick over correction by a relatively inexperienced driver, sending the car sideways into a telephone pole.

In the movie version, this is where the scene would cut to slow motion, eventually fading to black and coming back to eyes blinking open through a haze. Vision clearing to reveal a look around a sterile room filled with machinery. Beeping, whirring, clicking sounds. People flitting in and out, the protagonist soon to find out that he has been unconscious — comatose in fact — for four days. Instinctively trying to speak only to find the task impossible thanks to an endotracheal tube.

One of the first things I did after waking up in the hospital was to write a note to my Aunt Carly.

"When can I go back to your house? More comfy."

Most of the time that I spent in that hospital is a blur. I remember being extremely angry at all the stupid questions they kept asking me.

"Do you know what day it is?"

No. I have no fucking idea, I thought.

"Do you know where you are?"

In my head I was thinking, *Well, let me see here. You're wearing a lab coat and stethoscope, I have a fucking tube down my throat pumping air in me, and one in my side with a machine that is pumping fluid out of me 24/7. Let me take a wild fucking guess and say I am in a hospital.*

As a patient, I was a complete fucking asshole.

In writing this, I interviewed those who were around me at the time to get a better sense of how I must have felt, in the hopes of trying to paint a picture from the perspective of a young, helpless teen who had the misfortune to wake up unable to move. Clearly, this should have been the "turn my life around" moment I so desperately needed. Unfortunately, it appears the bitter reality of what I experienced is the one thing those witnesses can recall after 30 years. They tell an eerily similar story: "You were an angry young man who wanted nothing but to get the fuck out of that hospital."

I had been sent to Australia because I was an angry young man on a path of self-destruction. It should not surprise me that my near-death experience did not soften that anger. Instead it only served to fan the flames of the acrimony that had developed within me.

I'm fairly certain the nurses were not very happy when they did take the tube out of my throat and I could talk. I had matured in the months that I had been in Australia. I learned the value of hard work. I had my 17th birthday there. I wanted to believe I was as close to adulthood as I had ever been. Instead, I was a belligerent, know-it-all,

17-year-old asshole who had no understanding of what it meant to be grateful to even be alive.

At some point in that first week, my mother flew over from Canada to visit me, and I have to tell you that this little asshole had never been so happy to see his mommy in his entire life.

Max had lost control around a bend and hit a telephone pole at the edge of a cane paddock. Max's girlfriend was thrown out the vehicle window and landed relatively unscathed. Max was knocked around inside the vehicle. He ended up with a cracked rib or two and a ruptured spleen that had to be removed. He checked himself out of the hospital against doctors' orders shortly after his surgery.

Unfortunately for me, I received the worst of the injuries. I was thrown across the car and dented the car outward. My spleen was so badly ruptured that, if I had been 30 minutes later getting to the hospital, I would not have survived. Given the severity of the apparent internal bleeding that was going on, the doctors were forced to rip open my abdominal cavity with such reckless abandon in order to find out what was happening inside of me. When I look at my scar today that stems from belly button to sternum, I think of a scene from M*A*S*H where the surgeons are elbow deep in someone's guts covered in blood. On top of what turned out to be an emergency splenectomy, I also suffered a crushed lung and several broken ribs.

Another friend, Conrad, had been following us in his Ute (Australian slang for "utility," a small truck-like vehicle) with friends and came around the corner after we had already gone off the road. Conrad visited me in the hospital and recounted the story. When he saw the headlights in the cane paddock, he thought we were "playing silly buggers." In other words, he thought we were jacking around and trying to be funny, hiding the vehicle in the sugar cane field. If it had not been for them following us, I likely would not be here to tell you the tale today.

Fortunately, there was no brain damage (future decisions might still make you question this statement), even though I had been knocked unconscious and had stayed there for the better part of four days. I didn't realize how lucky I was to have survived and also not to remember any of the trauma that had occurred. Our brains have a way of protecting us that most of us will never comprehend.

Trauma Rewrites Our Brain

When it comes to trauma of any kind, our brains hold the power to rewrite things. This is an important concept to pay attention to. Our brains are complex; we still do not fully understand how they work. Memories are not always true or accurate. In the case of trauma our brains can easily block out chunks of time. This is a fairly well-accepted truth when it comes to things like car accidents, but likely not as well accepted for lesser events. Awareness of how our brains protect us in times of trauma is an important first step on the path to self-improvement. This holds true for events large and small. Trauma comes in many forms and not always as obvious as a car accident or any specific incident. It could come in the form of obvious traumatic events like war, physical injury, sexual abuse, domestic abuse, or the death of a loved one. But being bullied, the loss of a job, being overlooked for a promotion, being let down by a friend, emotional neglect: these traumatic events can be more subtle, potentially causing them to be more insidious.

Knowing that our perspective of events may be, and likely is, skewed to some degree allows us an opportunity to see things through an alternate lens. This perspective is useful when we want to challenge beliefs that do not serve us or when we are looking to heal from any traumatic event. If we attempt to treat the symptoms of these events without addressing the feelings themselves, we are setting ourselves up for failure.

At the time I was far too young or naive to really understand the ramifications of coming so close to the end of my life. But that

17-year-old boy thought he had lived a lifetime. He thought he knew more than most. He thought he was invincible, that life owed him. I'm fairly confident that even being knocked unconscious, losing a spleen, crushing a lung, and being placed on life support caused no immediate improvement of the emotional immaturity this young man demonstrated.

It seems unfathomable that I have lived more than 30 years since that time, almost two lifetimes of what I had maintained up until that point. To think my journey might have come to such an abrupt end at the ripe old age of 17 is horrifying and underscores the good fortune that I have managed to enjoy in my life. Perhaps the writing of this will assist me in being more empathetic with my own son, who at the time of this writing is the very age where I was sent off to live my fate, to tread the path that would lead me to where I am today.

Gratitude

My lack of gratitude in even surviving such an ordeal is very difficult to wrap my head around as an adult. I try to empathize with this young man and have a very difficult time doing so. He moved through the experience with a sense of anger and entitlement. It is a scene I still see played out today in my business life by immature people of all ages, whether a receptionist steals from you because that person feels entitled to a raise they are not receiving or an associate demands the highest levels of compensation while brand new and unproven in the business.

It may have taken 30 years, but I have come full circle. I have faced that young man in the mirror, and I have given him the stern talking to that he so desperately needed but refused to hear back then. When I think of my own son and my frustration for his lack of gratitude over the little things we do, like driving him to soccer or paying for his extracurricular activities, this pales in comparison to how those who helped save my life must have felt.

In his book *Slaughterhouse-Five*, Kurt Vonnegut gives the main character Billy Pilgrim the ability to become "unstuck in time," moving through life events with no consideration to time. How I long to become that version of Billy Pilgrim and become unstuck in time. I would go back and visit those who saved my life, those who received nothing but my scorn and disdain in doing so. I would go back and show them the version of the man that I have become today, and I would make them proud. I would show them what I'm doing to try and make a better world. I would ask their forgiveness and hope beyond hope that they would take some comfort, some 30 odd years later, that the thankless work they did back then has made a difference in this world.

I would assure those medical personnel that I will do whatever I can to shine my light bright in this world. I will be that "Man in the Arena" that Theodore Roosevelt so eloquently articulated in his 1910 address by the same name. Their work also ensured that two more bright souls, my offspring, will live to carry on the journey that I began and that they advance another day. I would assure them that I will carry on the work that they started back then, and I too will save lives. I too will make a difference in this world, that I too will strive to have an exponential effect on this planet that I occupy.

I would be grateful. I would be grateful, and I would demonstrate gratitude.

This is something on which we could all use a little work . I am almost positive at some point in your exposure to social media you have seen much talk about the benefits of gratitude. Though if you are like me, unless you are writing a book discussing gratitude, you likely gloss over it.

Dr. Robert Emmons, a leading expert on gratitude, outlines four major reasons why gratitude is good:

GRATITUDE ALLOWS US TO CELEBRATE THE PRESENT

Emotions are fleeting, short lived. Positive emotions crave change. We quickly adapt to positive life circumstances and move to a place where we take many positives for granted. Gratitude is about appreciating the value of something, shining a light on those positive events or things highlighting the value of them in our lives. When we can highlight the benefits, we are less likely to take these events for granted. When we actively seek the good in our lives, we become more engaged, allowing us to become participants and not simply spectators in our life.

GRATITUDE BLOCKS TOXIC, NEGATIVE EMOTIONS

The opposite of gratitude is entitlement, envy, regret, or resentment. Practicing gratitude makes it impossible to hold those conflicting emotions. There is much research on gratitude and its effects on reducing the frequency and duration of bouts of depression.

GRATEFUL PEOPLE ARE MORE STRESS RESISTANT

Dr. Emmons says "Gratitude builds up a sort of psychological immune system that can cushion us when we fall. Grateful people are more resilient to stress, whether minor everyday hassles or major personal upheavals."

GRATITUDE INCREASES YOUR SENSE OF SELF WORTH

Gratitude is an affirmation of goodness in our lives. It does not mean that our lives are perfect, nor does it mean that we do not legitimately have things to be unhappy about. As my mother (and Monty Python) used to say, "Always look on the bright side of life."

Clearly, there are times in our lives when it will be difficult to see the good. However, the practice of gratitude forces us to notice the positive things in our lives. If we build a habit of acknowledging the good when things are positive, we help ourselves immensely when the "shit hits the fan" and we truly need that perspective. It is, once again, all about awareness.

I took for granted the fact that I got to leave that hospital of my own volition. I did not have the insight or acumen to see how fortunate I was, and as a result I missed out on a phenomenal opportunity to practice gratitude.

When you first start to explore the concept of gratitude, it can be a little daunting. You might feel a little fraudulent at first. Let's face it: we can all make a list of things for which we are supposed to be grateful, right? But what does it mean to actually *feel* grateful? While I had no idea at 17, I understand the concept much better as an adult.

Gratitude also requires an acknowledgement that that goodness comes from somewhere outside of ourselves. For those of you who touch lives every day and who feel a lack of gratitude on the part of those you help, know this: you do make a difference, and while those you touch may not be fully aware, as was true for me, their gratitude may not manifest until many years down the road. Know that you will change the world with the work that you were sent to do. Each life you touch is an opportunity to touch others — two, three, or more down the line.

Little more than three weeks after Mom came to rescue me from the evil clutches of the horrific care that I was receiving in the Northern Australia hospital (seriously, those people were saints to put up with me), my journey Down Under came to an end. Mom had spent three weeks ferrying a young, arrogant ingrate back and forth twice a day to the hospital to receive his antibiotics and getting only one break from me to take in the wonders of the Great Barrier Reef with a visit to Dunk Island.

While Australia was a wonderful place to visit for a time, I felt a fair amount of unspoken relief in going home with my mother. The 18-hour flight wrapped up a four-month experience that would forever shape the path I would take. While I still appeared a hard, obstinate young man on the outside, the experiences of Australia had started to soften my soul, setting up a work ethic that would manifest immediately and some delayed gratitude that would take about three decades to acquire.

In the meantime, I had some killer stories to tell my friends back home.

Unfortunately, I also had a renewed sense of invincibility.

WHEN SOMETHING'S GOTTA CHANGE:

Taking time to reflect on what we are grateful for is a powerful practice. Expressing gratitude to those who have affected us can amplify that significantly.

For whom in your life are you grateful, both past and present?

____

____

____

____

How can you show or do more to show your gratitude to the people in your life who have stepped in when you needed them most?

____

____

____

____

CHAPTER 7

STILL INVINCIBLE

I would love to tell you that on the heels of my near-death experience in Australia I had an epiphany, that I made a conscious decision to turn my life around. I would love to tell you that I came home with a deep sense of freshly-instilled gratitude for being alive and a work ethic equal to the task of making my way in the world. I would love to tell you this, but sadly this is not the case. I was not that smart. To this day, I still refer to the Australia trip as THE turning point in my existence. The reality is that my 17-year-old invincible self really was not seeking the Truth at that point in my life. I clearly had it all figured out. I was content to await and fulfil the destiny that would surely be thrust upon me.

Perhaps if someone had challenged me directly to find the lessons in what I'd been through — telling me that I couldn't do it, daring me to push past my limited perspective — it would have bored through the thick layer of armour that I wore like a badge of honour. I'm not sure anyone could have gotten through to me at that point. I do know this: if you can find a way to open yourself to the lessons, your path will be clearer, less obstructed, and far less painful. At 17, I wasn't there yet.

I came back to Canadian soil and continued to move through life at breakneck speed.

It was shortly after returning home that I met Darren, who would go on to become one of my best friends through my teens and 20's. We met by way of our mutual friend Graham and little did we know that this trio of wannabe badasses would become the basis for a several-decades-long friendship.

Darren, Graham, and I had met up at a friend's and headed down the street to find a party. It was a warm spring evening, though I'm not sure any variance in weather would have changed the customary "uniform." If it had been cool enough, I might've worn my fleece plaid mac jacket under the requisite denim storm rider. This night was jeans, concert tee, high top sneakers, and the storm rider.

I'm not sure who brought what, but somehow we ended up with a giant-sized Big Gulp and a 2-6 of whiskey. We made our way down the street alternating swigs of whiskey and the soda, subtly daring each other with ever larger sips of whiskey and ever smaller slurps of soda.

A few blocks later, we found ourselves in a park with time to kill. As always, we were ever prepared for the party. It seems odd to me now thinking about how we managed to get anywhere or learn where the parties were, given the lack of connection compared to today. In any event, we ended up in a park with a crudely-assembled tree fort — basically just a platform up in the trees with a few two-by-fours nailed to the tree for ladder rungs.

In hindsight, climbing up a platform after powering back a bottle of whiskey was not a great idea.

The ideas got worse.

The objective for getting up into the fort was to find a secluded space to hot knife some hash. There must have been more efficient ways to get high. However, three teenagers carrying a blowtorch, a couple of kitchen knives, and a 2-liter pop bottle with the bottom cut off sure felt, in that moment, pretty fucking badass.

After we had done a couple hits of hash, somehow the conversation moved over to my recent Australia experience. I relayed the story of the car accident and how I was invincible and clearly a total rock star for having survived. I went on to show my groin-to-sternum "zipper," the scar that had been left after my emergency splenectomy. The wound had been sutured together with a series of staples, and you could still see the individual dots left by the staple holes. With all of us drunk and stoned, the sight of my belly zipper soon became the focal point of the evening.

In a spot on the top of the scar, underneath one of the staple dots, you could still feel a hard piece of something under the skin. I surmised that this was an errant staple that the doctors in their infinite wisdom had failed to remove. It was certainly an odd feeling and quite uncomfortable to the touch.

After a few minutes of us poking at this possible staple floating around underneath my skin, Darren came up with a brilliant idea.

He looked at me with a wide grin, holding up the red-hot hash knives. "We should cut it out!"

"Fucking right. It's a pain and I'd love to get rid of it. Go for it."

I lifted my shirt higher, exposing the "staple" for extraction by Dr. Darren. He came in slowly with the scorching tips, watching my face. When he got within an inch of my skin, seeing my expression stoic and intent, he dropped the bravado as well as the knives. He wrapped his arm around my neck, hugging my head into his.

"Dude, you're fucking nuts," he said, handing me the bottle of whiskey.

This was to become one in a series of similar idiotic scenarios after I got home. You might think that I would have been a little more cognizant of my own mortality after coming so close to death in Australia, but for me this was clearly not the case.

It's amazing the lessons we can miss when we're not open to or actively seeking our Truth. At this point in my life, though, I was not ready to face the possibility that I did in fact have lessons to learn from my experiences. Instead, I twisted my experiences to support the beliefs that I already had. My cognitive bias, supporting a traditional, societal stereotype of what a badass was, was strong.

At a 2017 talk I gave, a young man asked me whether or not a person had to actually live the "wrong way of thinking" in order to get to the *right* way of thinking.

My immediate answer was, "Of course not." If you can learn from someone else's mistakes, then why live them? This seems to be nothing but common sense, but as I reflect on that question in the context of my 17-year-old self, I'm not sure there was anything anyone could have said or done to make me bypass that portion of hard learning.

If a near-death car accident didn't push me to examine my life a little more closely, I'm not sure how any amount of preaching, lecturing, or otherwise would have reached me. I suppose you have to be open to receiving the lessons that life has to offer.

For most of us this is an extremely challenging task. We are not programmed to seek teachings through our adversities. While our brains protect us from trauma by rewriting the story, it takes immense effort to remain conscious through the teachings you might be receiving. We require vigilance, patience, and practice to recognize these moments, tune into them, and dissect the lessons. With practice our reactions eventually become honed, although it takes an immense amount of work to get there. One of the practices I now employ is to use the little phrases and internal dialog when negativity strikes as a cue to actively look for the lessons. Anytime I find myself something like, "Why me?" or "This isn't fair" I catch myself and instead start asking, "What can I learn from this?"

One would think that my experience abroad would have prepared me to examine and learn from my time there. It did not. Yet.

WHEN SOMETHING'S GOTTA CHANGE:

The events in our life and, more importantly, the lessons that we take from them, ultimately shape the human beings we become. We need to do the important work of looking back for the lessons.

What negative self-talk phrases can you use to anchor better questions?

____

____

____

____

Are you open to learning the lessons in your life, or do you still cling to the bravado of your experiences?

____

____

____

____

CHAPTER 8

WORK ETHIC

I'm not sure if it was the forced work in the land Down Under or an innate characteristic that simply had to be uncovered, but my work ethic did not diminish after arriving back in Canada. This work ethic is something on which I pride myself today, assuring myself that, despite a lack of any apparent natural talent, hard work will always carry me through. Regardless of the environment, despite the struggles of the marketplace, I always seem to find a way to rise above the turmoil — in fact, to ride it like a wave, to mobilize this force of nature to propel myself to new heights. This was a realization I had yet to make, and little did I know how important a lesson it would become.

In the months after my return to Canada, I had already fallen back into my old cycle of hanging out without purpose like the night in the tree fort. My natural tendency — everyone's — is to fall back to the status quo. I find great comfort in continuing with what I know, even when I know it does not serve me.

I did continue with the solid work ethic and find a job. My lack of education, my youth, and my haircut (think Bruce Dickinson from Iron Maiden) put me out of the running for any real job prospects at that point in my life. My life as a pump jockey was not glamorous, nor was my stint as a car wash attendant whose greatest joy was finding spare change on the floor of the cars he vacuumed out. Suffice it to say, while these entry-level jobs provided enough funding for Friday night beer and the odd bag of weed, they were not jobs that I could build into a career. Of course, at that point in my life, the idea of a career was not even close to being on my radar.

The 30- and 40-somethings who were my superiors at the car wash had little impact on me. I did not judge or despise them, or fear that that type of position would become my fate. Even with zero prospects, I knew in my heart of hearts that I was destined for bigger things.

Do you know that feeling?

It was this certainty that drove me. I was acknowledging and fanning the flames of this inner fire that kept me moving forward, knowing that there must be more to the life that I was currently living. I was also making the choice to accept this feeling as a challenge and a driver, as opposed to a depressant or downer. I was making the decision not only to *feel* like there was more but to actually *become* more. We all have this option — accepting the challenge and not the fear — available to us.

I knew in my heart of hearts I was destined for bigger things.

Bagging Shit

Sometime in 1986, I got wind of a stellar job opportunity. Of course, "stellar" at that point in my life was defined by the amount of beer I could buy per week on the offered pay. It was definitely a simpler time.

What kind of skill, talent, or specialized training did you need to bag potting soil, manure, and other items used to curate an abundance of breathtaking botanical brilliance? The answer, my friends, is none: zero skills required to attain the position of Soil Plant Worker at Greenleaf Garden Supplies. It was perfectly matched to my existing skill set. When I heard about this opportunity paying somewhere in the neighbourhood of $10 per hour, I was quick to put together a simple résumé and drop by an application. My, how things have changed. Now my 16-year-old waits until midnight, Googles the company with whom he is desirous of obtaining employment, fills out an online form, hits submit, goes back to playing Minecraft, and crosses his fingers that he gets a favourable response.

Once I was hired, I reported directly to the warehouse manager, Stan. As you may well imagine, the job was pretty straightforward. The soil plant tucked in the lower portion of the warehouse consisted of a loft with a large hopper used to blend ingredients into the final soil mix. There was a science to the madness. Each different type of soil had its own recipe, its own ratio of peat moss, perlite, vermiculite, sand, and/or bark mulch. There was potting soil, veggie mix, cactus mix, indoor and outdoor mix, and even a special mix particular to African violets.

A single set of stairs took you up to the loft area. Around the hopper, there was just enough room on the platform for the forklift to drop two skids of ingredients, the bulk of which was usually peat moss. We would have a few bags of perlite or vermiculite lined up against the wall opposite. Lifting the large hinged plywood lid covering the hopper revealed the large steel auger that went down the middle to mix the recipe like some kind of giant pancake mix.

Underneath the loft, a conveyor belt began with a variable height bag sealer and ended with a bag flattener, accompanied by a glue sprayer. The slight spray of glue on the back of the bag made certain that the stacked pallets remained intact for shipping to the various garden centres and greenhouses.

We rotated through three stations, requiring a minimum of two staff to keep the plant functional. Someone had to mix the soil up top in the hopper, someone else would bag it in whatever sized potting soil bag we happened to be making at the time, and a third person at the end of the line would pull the bags off after the glue spray and stack them on a pallet. In the event there were only two on shift, bagging would pause while we jointly mixed a new batch. In busy times, there might be up to four of us working the plant at a given time: one bagging, one stacking, one running the forklift moving completed skids, and one bringing fresh supplies up to the mixing loft. Each task had its perceived appeal, and tenure was typically the deciding factor on who got which job.

While the work could be extremely monotonous, we found ways to keep it somewhat interesting, like competitions to see if we could outdo a previous record for the number of skids of dirt bagged in a day. My competitive drive and my work ethic combined to make me a good soil plant worker — who knew? I'm certain Stan loved having me down in the soil plant because it was all systems go, and I set record after record in terms of the amount of soil bagged on a daily basis.

Sometimes we have to do the things we least desire to become the man we are most meant to be

At that time for me it was really just about making a tedious job somewhat interesting, but turning tasks into competitions against my own personal records is a pattern of behaviour that has followed me in the years since.

We are often told that we are to "follow our passion," and while I would never tell you to quell your passion, I do wonder about the wisdom of this advice. Typically, the story goes that at the age of 17 or 18, you should find what it is that makes you happy (what you are passionate about) and find a career in that arena. If we set our hopes on finding our overarching passion and building a career around that, we risk being sadly disappointed in the event that that is not happening at an acceptable pace. If, instead, we change our focus from finding our passion and building a career around it to looking at our career and finding what we can get passionate about within it, that bodes far better for us. Our passions early in life change over time and are often not the emotional drivers in our 30s, 40s or 50s. Experimentation is the key.

For me, I was passionate about improvement. I could find plenty of opportunity within the soil plant to foster that passion. I can vividly recall tweaking processes and procedures to improve efficiency. Our stacker had to be moving fast enough that the bags did not pile up in the shallow six-foot square bin at the end of the production line. From time to time we would bag large deliveries of steer manure into smaller bags. Who was on the forklift at what time and how could we maximize production without getting backed up at the bagging hopper?

Eventually this work ethic started to yield dividends for me. One of the easiest and most coveted jobs at the soil plant involved catching a ride on one of the delivery trucks. In the busy season when loads were large and there were numerous items to unload at each stop, the drivers would sometimes take one of us to be a "swamper" and help unload. It was a great job for a few reasons. You got to get out of the warehouse, you only had to work at the stops, you could sit and shoot the shit with the drivers in between, and you were usually out all day, killing your entire workday.

I recognized very early that the drivers chose who they took with them when they headed out on their daily route. Although I could not have defined it at the time, I started to learn the value of relationship building. I realized that people tend to want to hang around people they liked.

Relationship building rule number one: "Don't be an asshole." The second thing I noticed is that the drivers were more likely to select the individual who most lightened their workload. As a swamper, at every stop I was out the door sometimes even before the truck came to a complete stop. I would sprint back to the rear, open the roll doors, climb up, and start pulling out the order specific to the given shop where we were. For small orders this often meant that the driver did not even have to set foot out of the cab. It wasn't long before they moved me out of the soil plant and into the warehouse picking orders.

We all have choices. You can stay stuck where you are, or you can choose to change your circumstances.

A combination of hard work, persistence, and asking the right questions about advancement meant that after a few years in the warehouse, I obtained my Class 3 driver's license. After a stint as a substitute driver, I was ultimately given my own truck. Imagine the feeling I now had: I was the one who got to choose which swampers rode with me.

Eventually I had moved through the ranks as far as I was likely to go within the warehouse. I yearned for a greater challenge. The only place left to go was up. Literally. The sales offices were right above the warehouse, and I set my sights on getting out of the warehouse altogether.

I'm not really certain if it was sales specifically that was calling me or whether I was simply suffering through another bout of squirrel syndrome (think of Dug the Dog from the movie *Up*). I made the decision to talk to Stan and ask him whether there might be an opportunity in the sales department. I was still young, in my early

20s, and had an awful lot to learn, but I had proven my reliability over my four years in the warehouse and felt that I had a pretty good shot at advancing.

Never one to thrive on confrontation of any sort, I was extremely nervous about having the conversation with Stan. Much to my delight, I did not spontaneously combust. Stan was quite receptive, and I felt very positive that something would come my way.

About a month after the conversation, when nothing had yet happened, it dawned on me that Stan had no motivation whatsoever to move me out of the warehouse. I was one of the hardest-working labourers Greenleaf had down there, and with the amount of turnover we had, I would certainly be hard to replace. I decided that I needed to have that conversation again, only this time I would do it with Al, the sales manager. I asked him directly if there might be an opportunity for a young up-and-comer to take on a role in the sales department.

Al immediately started me one day a week with all the "shit" accounts that none of the other sales guys wanted, but I did not care. I had my foot in the door. That was all that really mattered.

Eventually, a full-time sales position landed me a company car and gas card.

I. Had. Arrived.

I still get a kick out of recounting the beginnings of my work life. Yes, I literally started my career bagging shit. It is something in which I take great pride to this very day. There should never be a job that is beneath you, a job that you're too good to do. If it needs to get done, simply make it happen. Stop the excuses. Stop the bullshit — pardon my pun — and take a step forward. Whether that step is large or small, you can always move forward.

This was the big time as far as I was concerned. Given where I had started, I was pretty pleased with the progress that a little hard work had ensured for me.

As you may well have imagined by now, I have a bit of a pattern. Success will only tie me down for so long before I start looking for that next big thing. It soon became abundantly clear to me that I was not going to become the businessman I knew I was destined to be by hawking garden supplies.

The lessons for me in those years were the same as a popular book and a mantra that I use while running ultra-marathons: "Relentless forward progress." No matter the obstacle, no matter the setback or hardship, find a way to keep moving forward.

We all have the ability to give everything we have within us at any given time. Even when we feel it is not enough, we still have the choice to move forward or not.

For me, this was the easy part of the lessons yet to come. Little did I know how much my commitment to forward progress would be tested.

WHEN SOMETHING'S GOTTA CHANGE:

Sometimes we have to do the things that we least desire to become the man we are most meant to be.

What can you find in your work right now that you can get passionate about?

____

____

____

____

What steps can you take, large or small, right now to move forward in your life?

____

____

____

CHAPTER 9

BEYOND THE COMFORT ZONE

Enter Frank Biller. I'm not sure who originally introduced us, but I met him at our recreational league hockey. We were a Division 8 team more adept at drinking beer post-game than we ever were on the ice. I really don't know how Frank ended up on our team. He was hands down our best player, having once played for the British Columbia Hockey League's New Westminster Royals, and he had been the leading scorer on the Merritt Centennials in 1987 and 1988.

Frank's charm and talents on the ice soon made him a leader in the dressing room. He was the cool kid on the block, a hierarchy that endured well past high school for us, just a bunch of 20-something weekend warriors and wannabe hockey players. Always quick with a story or joke, his collegial manner made him a favourite to be around. On the ice, he was a marvel to watch. Not overly fit, but with hands like velvet, he never gave you the chance to remove the puck from him even if you were able to catch him.

It was a bit of an embarrassment, as he clearly did not belong in the same league as the rest of our team, some of whom only learned to skate as adults. He was the guy who, on the bench, would ask you where you wanted him to score and then follow it up next shift with a deliberately-placed goal to match. At the Penalty Box Pub after games, he was always the one to regale us with the most colourful and interesting stories imaginable. His tales of semi-pro hockey life left us wanting more all the time.

Frank always had a smile on his face and was quick with a joke and the essence of good-natured locker room ribbing. There's a fine line between the classroom bully and the good-natured jokester who can pick equally on the jock, the nerd, or the quiet kid in the corner without offending. Frank's teasing never came across as malicious, and he spread it around just enough that it wasn't targeted at any specific individual. On any given night, we were all subject to become victim to his sharp wit.

There was something about Frank that was simply magnetic. He had a way about him that made you want to please him, and there was an innate leadership quality that he was clearly learning to hone.

As I got to know Frank over the following weeks and months, I started to learn about his business endeavours. Frank was a self-employed mortgage broker. Back in 1994, the market and expectations for mortgage brokers were substantially different than they are now. Ever the prolific embellisher, Frank spun tales of his business acumen that were far beyond anything that actually happened, although I'm certain he never used the term "mortgage broker" in any of the conversations we had.

Whatever it was that he was doing, it seemed clear to me that he was the epitome of a *real* businessman. In all honesty, for a then 24-year-old who'd spent the last six years earning just enough to pay rent and the bar tab, it probably didn't take much to achieve that title in my mind.

I've recounted the tale of how I got into the mortgage business many times over the years. Rarely do I give the story in its entirety, as I'm about to do; I can usually sum it up with the following: "I played hockey with a guy who was a broker. It looked like he was having fun and making lots of money, so I asked him, 'What do you have to do to do that?'"

The rest, I tell them, is history.

Frank told me that to do what he did — raising money for syndicated mortgages — I needed to have a mortgage broker's license. When I probed further, he went on to explain that I would need to take a course offered by the University of British Columbia's Real Estate division.

Since I'd already decided my days as a garden supply salesperson were numbered, I did a little investigation, and fortunately for me, the course could be taken via correspondence. There were no prerequisites whatsoever, a very good thing considering my illustrious school career had peaked at the completion of Grade 9 and was non-existent after that. There was still a slight problem: The course was somewhere in the neighbourhood of $1,200 and I was perpetually into my $1,000 overdraft protection.

Have I mentioned what a wonderful man my father Dave is? In a decision he would later come to regret, Dad financed — or, rather, donated — my passage into the business world. As a career educator and then high school guidance counsellor, he must have found the prospect of his misguided, eldest child going back to school extremely appealing — and to a legitimate, big name, fully-accredited university.

Okay, maybe I am overreaching. It was, after all, a single course being delivered via correspondence to a high school dropout. I can assure you, though, that when I sent in that registration cheque and subsequently received the course material, I felt sure I was on my way to something much larger.

The course lasted nine months, and my productivity at Greenleaf went down substantially during that time. I had checked out, already mentally moving on to my next adventure, and I didn't have the maturity to do what was right and continue wholeheartedly until I was officially done in my current position. I put in my time and did what I needed to do to get by, but I didn't put in the same amount of effort I had previously. I don't know if this is just me, or if this is simply a human characteristic.

The correspondence course taught a lot of math, something that was right up my alley. Although I would eventually come to realize this was a highly misguided belief, I believed myself to be unquestionably more logical than creative.

As the short version goes, I asked Frank what I had to do in order to do what he did, then I did it and asked him what came next. I will never forget our conversation after I finished the course and approached him about my possible next steps.

The first thing he said to me was, "I'm proud of you."

It's not an entirely normal thing for a peer to say, especially not during the years when we were starting to splash around the edge of the waters of manhood. I'm sure this is a phrase my parents said to me time and time again, yet somehow, coming from Frank, a peer whom I respected and wanted to emulate, the impact was profound.

I have kept those five little words — *I am proud of you* — close at hand, and I look for the opportunity to use them whenever I can because of the power they had on me.

As we discussed what my possible next steps , I confess that I still really didn't know what I was getting myself into. All I knew was that he was having lots of fun and by all accounts I would make lots of money.

Frank suggested that my next step, with his assistance, would be to set up a meeting with the owner of the company where he worked.

While he couldn't promise anything, it would be a start. The meeting would take place the following week at their downtown office.

The next week passed slowly for me; I felt a strange combination of excitement and trepidation. While I had graduated from soil plant to sales, I had still been in a fairly blue-collar industry. I hadn't had the opportunity to take meetings at downtown offices with executives of companies. The thought of having an interview at such an office with such an individual was, frankly, terrifying, but I seemed to have a desire to put myself in extremely uncomfortable situations in an effort to germinate personal growth.

These types of situations would become, and continue to be, fertile grounds for me to grow into the exact person I hoped to become.

When the day finally arrived, I dressed myself in the finest garment I owned at the time: a $100 suit that I got on sale for two-for-one. I hopped in my car, heart beating faster than after a set of Tabata drills, and set off downtown to find the offices of Brian Slobogian.

I vividly remember walking up to the building and wiping the sweat from my palms onto my trousers, wondering how I was going to get through the handshake without a spray of sweat flying everywhere and effectively ending the interview before it had even begun.

Once I get my heart set on something, everything else pales.

Over the years, one of the lessons I've tried to learn is to follow my heart. I make an effort to reduce the amount of time I spend doing something that my heart is not really into. I mean, after all, why waste precious time in a place where your heart is not?

I understand there are reasons that may keep you in less than ideal situations, but my hope is that you're actively working to remove yourself from those circumstances. I will continue to discuss self-limiting beliefs throughout this book. Start thinking about some of the beliefs you hold that don't serve you well.

As I write and reflect it makes me wonder how often we use these words with ourselves. How many times do you tell yourself that you are "proud" of you? Are there things in your life of which you should be proud? If not, are there things in your life you should be changing so that you can become proud of yourself?

I walked into the office without a clue that this would be the beginning of a career lasting several decades, bringing some of the best and worst experiences of my life.

WHEN SOMETHING'S GOTTA CHANGE:

Growth happens at the edge of our comfort zone. Being intentional about putting yourself in uncomfortable positions can be a massive catalyst for growth.

What terrifying or uncomfortable situations have you put yourself into as you pursued a goal?

____

____

____

____

Even if the outcome wasn't what you wanted, how did the experience affect you?

____

____

____

____

CHAPTER 10

BECOMING A BUSINESSMAN

The mortgage office was not what you would call grand by any stretch of the imagination. It was a good thing I really had nothing to compare it to, or I would have been disappointed. At that moment in time, I'm certain we could have met in a back alley and I would have still been in awe. Remember that feeling when you move from elementary school to junior high school? Junior high wasn't really all that impressive, but I was just so thrilled to be moving on from Buckingham Elementary that Edmonds Junior High seemed palatial in comparison.

While not a 100-story glass high-rise, the office building was nice and located in downtown Vancouver, which held a lot of mystique for me. The office of Brian Slobogian and Frank Biller was a simple, single room, no more than a few hundred square feet. One wall was lined with a counter with an array of phones, fax machines, and copiers spread out among a few workspaces.

When Frank opened the door, he greeted me with a warm smile, putting a finger to his lips as I entered, indicating that I should be quiet because Brian was on the phone.

It's funny to think back on this scene that I thought so grand at the time, so much so that it had me a nervous wreck with sweaty palms and butterflies in my stomach, feeling like I could puke at any moment. Today, if I walked into a similar scene with any prospect of a business relationship, I would turn around at the door. The experiences I have had over the past two decades have made me much more attuned to my gut and certainly much more apt to listen to such feelings.

Brian's gruff manner on the phone was right out of a scene from *The Wolf of Wall Street, Boiler Room*, or something akin to Alec Baldwin's character in *Glengarry Glen Ross*, without Baldwin's charm or good looks.

I was extremely intimidated and don't remember any of the interview. All I know is that, somehow, I walked out of that office with a job offer. I was thrilled to learn that I would be given a chance to earn my keep. I like to think that I put on an air of confidence and an impressive demeanour, but the more plausible scenario is that I was a young, pliable mind that could be moulded and shaped in a manner conducive to larger business plans.

My enthusiasm was soon tempered with the realization that I would now have to face Al, my sales manager at the soil plant, and let him know that I had decided to take my employment elsewhere. Never a big fan of confrontation, I somehow kept putting myself into these situations that required it.

Al took the news very graciously, even going so far as to tell me that, while he never did this for exiting employees, he would keep the door open for me. If things didn't work out as I expected, I was always welcome to come back — a lesson in making a favourable impression and not burning any bridges. Al's assurance gave me a lot of comfort as I moved forward on my journey. I was 25 years old, and I had just left the most stable job I'd ever had in my life – one that spanned almost eight years.

I moved full steam ahead, and within a few weeks I was a licensed mortgage broker working for the young start up Eron Mortgage Corporation, basically the third man in, and opportunity bound. Things moved fairly quickly after that.

I was brought in to listen to the two men on the phone and learn the tricks of the trade. My job would be to solicit investments in syndicated mortgages. I would later learn that the reason we were able to solicit investments the way that we did was because of an exception in the Securities Act. It allowed for the raising of capital for mortgages by way of sophisticated investors, without the need for an offering memorandum or prospectus, more complicated financial documents used to describe the inherent risks in investing. We used an instrument called a "Declaration of Trust," a much simpler document that outlined the participation in the mortgage being syndicated. This meant that if we had to raise a million dollars for a financing project, we could do so with ten investors at $100,000 apiece or 100 investors at $10,000 apiece.

The combination was immaterial, the sales pitch simple.

That first week in the office was an overwhelming whirlwind. I had no idea what I was doing, and I was being taught by individuals I didn't know well. Frank was fearless on the phone, and I spent most of that time simply listening to him solicit investments from prospective clients.

The company had purchased a list of presumably high net worth individuals. These lists came to us as bound books listed alphabetically by company. The information presented included the organization name, address, phone number, and a list of their top executives. We would then systematically go through and cold call CEOs, VPs, and other high-level executives with the standard pitch.

I can still rattle off most of the spiel they taught me:

"Hi, my name is Mike Cameron with Eron Mortgage, and I'm wondering if you would be interested in learning about earning a 12-18% return on investment secured by real estate?" I'd ask. The rate of return was substantially higher than most market securities at the time, although truth be told, I had no idea about any alternate investments. I was not qualified as an investment advisor, but I did believe in the solidity of the real estate asset that backed the investments we sought. In theory, the concept was a no brainer.

As a 24-year-old "businessman" I was certainly in awe of the mechanics of this operation. I watched eagerly and learned voraciously. Even now, as I look back, it was truly a remarkable thing. The three of us would cram into this tiny office day after day, my only role to support Frank and Brian.

I was stunned at the number of calls Frank could bang out in a day. He had absolutely zero "call reluctance." Frank was clearly the master of the cold call, with Brian masterminding deal after deal.

I will never forget one time in the office when Frank had a "live one" on the phone. We could only hear one side of the conversation, but this prospect was clearly making all the right noises. Frank was answering a plethora of questions, attempting to earn the trust — and money — of whomever was on the other end of the line.

It quickly became clear that Frank was simply making shit up as he went along. Brian, who overheard part of the conversation, rolled his chair over to Frank and gruffly said, "No, no, no! Give me that," yanking the phone out of Frank's hand and taking over the conversation.

I can only imagine my humiliation if I had been making that call. Yet somehow this was just business to both Frank and Brian; neither seemed to think there was anything out of the ordinary about the scenario.

And this was my new boss.

What did I know? Maybe this was how it was done. Maybe Frank deserved to be treated like an idiot. Perhaps this was how a businessman did things in 1994 in downtown Vancouver.

The scene was the first of several red flags I should have seen.

WHEN SOMETHING'S GOTTA CHANGE:

Paying attention to the world around you and heeding the warning signs can help move us forward in our pursuit of purpose.

What red flag warnings have you seen in hindsight that you didn't notice in the heat of the moment?

____

____

____

____

What are some of the warning signs that are in front of you right now?

____

____

____

____

CHAPTER 11

WHAT'S ON THE SCORECARD?

We didn't stay in that little downtown office for long. Success led to opportunity and opportunity meant expansion. We soon moved into the Kilborn Building located right at Burrard and Pacific in Vancouver. The office was still modest, but it was a step above the diminutive one-room station in which Eron had started. We were all keeping score of how far we had come, and moving into a bigger office was just one more victory we could record on our scorecards.

Frank and Brian now had individual offices, and Frank's wife Michelle came to work with me in the backroom, where she and I had the bullpen-type setup to ourselves. My main focus remained finding investors for deals. From time to time, Frank would bring back a "term sheet" on a deal and tell us that we needed X amount for a specific project. My job was to call as many people as necessary until the deal was fully funded. It was dialling for dollars in the most literal sense of the term.

I had no idea how great a training ground this was for me at the time. I quickly learned that some calls went well, and other calls were downright horrific. You had to have a pretty thick skin to pick up the phone time and time again with the high probability of rejection in this line of work. More than the lessons I learned about how to engage a prospect on the phone, the practice I was able to obtain was, in my opinion, better than any Harvard education I could have received. I had limited education, so the only way to compensate for that was by action, repetition, and experience.

Now, I'd love to tell you that I was a bear with the phone, systematically blowing through the lead directory in an effort to earn my keep. The truth is, I had to overcome an enormous amount of fear to make each and every call. But while I hated the call itself, I loved the reward when you had a successful call. I continually convinced myself that the next call would be *the* call that would get me that sale and gain me that commission. I also was able to frame the negative experience calls as learning experiences, understanding that sales is a numbers game. The more "no"s you get, the closer you come to a "yes."

Action outdoes experience. You can make up for a lot by moving forward regardless of your experience, skill, or ability.

One of my most memorable calls was with an individual who, while somewhat responsive, was not responding in the way I had hoped. By this time, maybe six months into this career, I could usually tell which way a call was going to go the instant the person on the other end of the line answered the call. This particular contact answered with a cranky "WHAT?!" His tone and demeanour basically screamed, *Why are you bothering me?*

I jumped into my scripted opening (which still sounded and felt very much like a scripted opening the way I said it) and waited for his response, fully expecting him to hang up.

He didn't.

Instead he responded, in what can only be described as a rough, grating voice, "Are ya lookin' for money or givin' it away?"

I was taken aback. This was the first time I had been asked this question, and being the badass businessman that I was, I saw an opportunity and I wasn't going to squander it.

Certainly, my job was to do the "looking for money" part, but, without the other end of the equation, all of the money in the world was moot. I stammered out a response, until he unleashed again.

"Are you fucking looking for money, or are you fucking giving it away?!"

I explained that, as brokers, we managed both sides of the transaction and that if he was interested, I could have someone contact him about getting him some financing. He launched into a lengthy diatribe about the uselessness of my skin, something about my mother, and the collapse of the Canadian financial system. Only then did he proceed to hang up on me.

Rattled, I put the phone down and looked up to see Frank standing at the other end of the space with a wide, boyish grin pasted on his face. "How'd that one work out for you?"

"Fuck you." I smiled back at him.

A typical day at the office: some boyish banter, some comparing of assholes to whom we'd spoken, and a fair amount of celebrating successes and new tallies on our scorecards.

I was eager, enthusiastic, and determined to light the world on fire. I had entered a new business about which I had no idea and in which I had no experience at all, but it was okay, because I was destined for greatness.

They say that knowledge is power. To that I generally say, "Bullshit." I was living the lesson that knowledge is only part of the equation. Knowledge without action is simply the passage of time. I was taking action. I was making things happen.

That same year, Tony Robbins was coming to Vancouver with his

Unleash the Power Within workshop. Three full days with Tony and a bonus half day if you wanted to stick around to hear him talk about health. I had been following Tony's work for years, and just when I was starting a new career, he was going to be appearing live in my hometown! It was amazing, and exciting, except for one little problem: money. I think the cost was something in the neighbourhood of $750 — an amount that I did not have. But I was not to be denied. Fortunately for me, I was a resourceful young man and determined to find a way to do it.

I considered my parents, but I had already tapped them for the cost of the course I needed to become a mortgage broker.

Maybe a loan from a friend? Nope, my friends were about as broke as I was. Most nights we managed to find a home for much of what we earned at the local pub or nightclub.

What about my new boss? Hmm... Now there was an interesting idea. I mean, after all, anything I learned at the conference would benefit him by way of increased performance. Asking Brian would be bold. Brian was a very quiet, gruff, abrupt, and extremely intimidating man — one of the sternest men I had ever met. He didn't talk a lot, but when he did, he commanded attention.

Who am I kidding? He was an asshole.

I mustered up all my courage the next morning and wandered over to Brian's corner office overlooking English Bay, more spacious than useful, with a large granite desk between him and whomever his audience was. When I say "large" desk, I mean its size required a crane to lift it to the window of his office and bring it in through the removed glass. That slab of granite was far too massive to be brought up the elevator or stairs.

He was *that* guy. And I had decided to ask him for a loan.

I sheepishly stuck my head in the door and gave the door frame a timid rap. Brian looked up over his reading glasses from his intent examination of what was likely some kind of multi-million-dollar development financing proposal. As usual, he had a scowl on his face and looked annoyed.

I asked if he had a few minutes, to which he replied, "Sure, sit down," nodding toward one of the chairs in front of his desk. I took a deep breath, entered his office, and quickly ran through my prepared Tony Robbins seminar sales pitch.

I focused on why I would like to go and why I thought there would ultimately be value for the organization in my attendance. He listened quietly, just sitting there staring at me. I had been done for what was probably only a matter of seconds before he responded, but the wait felt like an eternity.

Eventually, he reached over to open a desk drawer, pulled out a cheque book, took his Mont Blanc pen out of his suit pocket, and said, "How much?"

I replied, "$750," and then I sat with an awkward pause before blurting out "plus tax!"

He wrote out the cheque, leaned over his desk, and started sliding it across the desk to me.

Phew! What a relief. I visibly relaxed and reached out to grab the funding that was going to allow me to *unleash my power within,* but just as my hand was about to touch that life-altering piece of paper, he stopped and pulled it back to his side of the desk, looking me square in the eye.

"You know, Mike, learning is all well and good, but at some point, you just have to do"

Then he slid the cheque across the desk again. I thanked him profusely and slunk out of his office.

That day will stick with me for the rest of my life. Partly because I was scared shitless asking for the money, but largely because the reality of his words sank in that day.

All of that knowledge without action would simply be passing time.

As we became more successful at raising funds and financing projects, it appeared that the allure of becoming a broker exponentially increased. The cachet of the potential six-figure income was extremely compelling, and we started to see more and more individuals come onboard in a fundraising capacity. The office quickly filled with more of our testosterone-fuelled hockey friends, eager to find the approval of the charismatic young Frank.

If you had any connections with money, there was an opportunity for you to do well. In hindsight, I realize there was zero cost for the organization to bring in individuals who had any prospect of funnelling money in the door. We were all paid entirely through commissions, and we didn't earn anything if we didn't produce. We didn't cost the company anything other than desk space, paper clips, and printer paper.

Eron's growth over the next couple of years was surreal. As we grew in broker body count, you could see a pattern emerging: young, bold, beautiful people were at every desk. We kept knocking out walls and expanding the square footage of the office. The cars started getting fancier, and the lunches, cocktails, and cigars at fine dining restaurants became longer, more expensive, and more frequent.

I was indeed starting to feel like a real businessman.

It was around this time when I decided that I needed to up my game to enhance my businessman persona. In 1996, Porsche introduced the Boxster, a two seat mid-engine roadster that some called "the poor man's Porsche" because of its relatively low retail price. At that time, you couldn't have purchased any other model of Porsche for under six figures, but the Boxster started at $65,000.

Frank had decided that he was going to buy one for his wife.

I decided to buy one for myself.

I spent a few days down at the local dealership, but the model was in very high demand. I added my name to what was described to me as a long wait list. I'm not sure if that was bullshit or if I just got lucky, but within a few weeks I got the call that two cars, a yellow model and a silver version, had come in. Frank's wife had been waiting for the silver model. Yellow really wasn't something that I had contemplated, but I agreed to come down and have a look.

When I took it for a test drive, I was completely enthralled with the Porsche experience. If you've ever had the privilege of driving a Porsche, you know exactly what I'm talking about. A two-seat, canary yellow convertible that sticks to the road like it's on rails had every head in Vancouver turning. This was a new model, and as far as I knew, the only yellow one in Vancouver at the time.

I was 100 percent sold.

I will admit that I was a little nervous about how I was actually going to pay for it, but, hey, you gotta fake it 'til you make it, right? The lesson Brian had imparted about "sometimes you've just got to do" was ringing in my ears as justification.

I think my income for the last two years at that time had been $33,000 and $65,000 respectively. That's not a lot when you are looking at buying a vehicle that costs more money than you have ever seen in your life.

I remember discussing it with my dad, who was ever walking the balance of being a supportive father and screaming, *What the heck are you doing, son?!* at the top of his lungs. I'm sure my mind was well made up before I went to talk to him. To his credit, Dad listened to my justifications and merely said something to the effect of, "It's a beautiful vehicle. It's only slightly more expensive than my first house" — words of wisdom that this young upstart was too stupid to comprehend.

Back at the dealership, I sat with the finance manager and talked about lease options, though I really did not give a rip about anything other than driving off the lot with that vehicle. I had recently closed a substantial capital transaction and had received the biggest paycheque of my life, earning a total of $24,500. I used $10,000 of that for a down payment on the Porsche. I think they took my previous year's earnings into account when they approved my financing, but I suspect it wouldn't really have mattered. All they needed to know was that they had my deposit, I had insurance on the vehicle, and if I defaulted, they would keep my $10,000 and repossess my Boxster.

It was the most exciting — and stupidest — purchase I had ever made.

Driving a Porsche helped me feel more like one of the "boys" at the office, people my age who were all about living large. As was typical in my life, I bounced around the fringe of the "cool kids," never quite fitting in. The same held true at the office. I certainly developed some strong friendships over the years, but I still found myself seeking the approval of the inner circle, of "Biller and his boys."

While I was one of the originals, I was never one of the favourites, never one of the cool kids. So I was thrilled when my Eron colleagues invited me on a golf trip to Calgary, Alberta. Not exactly a high-end destination trip, but a trip nonetheless and one on which I had been invited to go. As avid golfers, they had expensive memberships to exclusive clubs and trips to destination resorts. This was to be a quick in-and-out weekend trip, comprised of 36 holes of golf over Saturday and Sunday.

After flying out to Calgary on Friday, we set up at a hotel that was nothing much to speak of. I'd expected to be able to tell tales of staying at the fanciest of hotels, drinking champagne, and dropping hundred-dollar bills, but this simply wasn't the case for this trip.

After a few rounds of golf on Saturday, we headed out to a nightclub, boys on the prowl. For the guys, the weekend was very much about the scorecard — both on the golf course and at the nightclub. It was about nothing more than conquest and victory, and I wanted desperately to score well. The club was hopping, and we were on top of the world after a great day of golf and a nice dinner, with a few beers in our bellies. Being strangers in a strange town, we had a clean slate, and the guys made up different personas to impress the women in the club, turning it into a competition. One was an architect in from Vancouver on business, another claimed to be a bigtime property developer. Who could come up with the most elaborate, yet plausible story became part of the scorecard.

I was running with the pack that I now wish to eliminate completely.

I'm embarrassed to admit that I was running with the kind of pack that I now hope to see become completely eradicated, the type of men who need to become extinct, and I hope this book will assist in that effort. I still find it hard to truthfully write some of these words, because I am ashamed of being complicit in what I now deem irresponsible. I'm disgusted to think of what I used to believe it meant to be a man. Here was a group of young, good-looking guys, loaded with charm, charisma...and with zero integrity. And I was dying to be a part of their club.

Fortunately for me, the values with which I had been raised meant that I realized I had been playing off someone else's scorecard. In the next few years I would endeavour to check off the things I thought important. Yet I still had a lot to learn about what truly matters.

WHEN SOMETHING'S GOTTA CHANGE:

Understanding what we value and therefore place on our personal scorecards requires deliberate reflection.

What are the values that are most important to you?

____

____

____

____

How do you use those values to guide the decisions you make?

____

____

____

____

CHAPTER 12

CHRISTINE AND THE ART OF NEW BEGINNINGS

In my twenties, I worked hard and I played hard, always keeping an eye out for that perfect match — the woman who would make my heart sing, the one who would make all the hard work worth the effort. I searched hard for her. There was nary a bar that I didn't check to see if she frequented.

Okay, truth be told, I was having *too* much fun sowing my wild oats during those years, yet at times I found it very lonely. Don't get me wrong, I wasn't exactly a player. But I did explore a lot of (ultimately unsatisfying) options at that time in my life.

So when, at the age of 28, I finally met "the one," I can assure you I was very excited, and relieved all at the same time.

Christine had been one of my brother Darryl's best friends for a number of years. They had met in university while she was dating one of Darryl's friends. I had met Christine a few times over the years at various functions and parties. I had always found her attractive, and she was incredibly sweet and kind. So when I heard through the grapevine that she and her longtime boyfriend had recently split up, my curiosity was piqued. Unfortunately, she and I did not often run in the same circles, and I did not even have her phone number at that point. At the time, I assumed we were not destined to be — until the day I went into my local Fitness World in downtown Vancouver and found her working at the fitness assessment desk, helping members do measurements and body fat ratios.

Fate, indeed, was on my side. As luck would have it, there was a spin bike beside her desk used for fitness testing. If she didn't have a client with her when I went in, I would make my way over and use the bike beside her and visit. This went on for a few weeks before I mustered up the courage to ask her out on a date. We ended up at Milestones restaurant, and I was well on my way to domestic bliss.

Now, I don't mean to say that this was all some cold, calculated master plan that I simply flicked a switch to execute, but when I look back, I realize that I was thinking, "This is the right time for me to settle down." I had always envisioned having kids early in life so that, as they grew, I would still have my youth to do fun things with them.

Twenty-eight was still fairly young, but I had a lot of life experience behind me to draw from, too. When Christine, whom I had been dating for just under a year, took a seven-week trip to China with her brother, I realized how much I wanted to be with her. In fact, I started a journal and wrote to her in it daily. This was in 1997, before email was readily accessible, and there were very few methods of communicating with her across the globe, with the exception of the rare, hyper-expensive phone call.

The day after her return to Canada, I proposed.

I did it up big and arranged for a skywriter to do a flyover of English Bay beach in downtown Vancouver at a set time. I knew that Christine had specific requirements for an engagement ring, so

I opted for the "traditional" Ring Pop candy ring so we could shop together later.

With my brother on board as surreptitious photographer, I set out to make the proposal happen. The flyover was a thrilling moment, and no police officers were alarmed by my brother lurking in the bushes with a camera. In the end, she said yes, and we had a fun memory to share at our wedding reception.

Now you may be asking yourself, how did this thrill-seeking badass wannabe go from clubbing and Porsches to marriage and kids?

Success

My idea of success wasn't just limited to career success. In my mind, a "real" successful man also had a gorgeous wife, perfect kids, and a house that was the envy of the neighbourhood. I wouldn't say I was exactly ready to have kids and the responsibilities of a family, but I've always believed that you can't wait until you're 100 percent ready to act. Sometimes, you just have to go for it. It would seem that Brian's earlier words "learning is all well and good, but at some point you've just got to do" would also guide my family life.

This was the first time in my life I felt "Imposter Syndrome".

Did I mention that I asked my future wife to move away from everyone she knew and start completely over in a new city right before we got married? Yeah, there's that. The beautiful thing about being in love is that it doesn't really matter where in the world you are, right?

After Eron financed two major projects in the province of Alberta, I realized there was a lot of opportunity for development financing and volunteered for the opportunity to set up shop there. I didn't really know what an Alberta location would look like or even exactly where that would be. When I made the decision to accept the role, there was no formal offer in place, no letter of intent, no real understanding of expectations or deliverables. All I knew was that at 28 years old, I was finally going to become the businessman — and family man — I knew I was destined to become.

As luck would have it, we had financed an office building in Edmonton, so the fates would have me travelling north as well as east. I was a complete neophyte to living anywhere outside my bubble of the lower mainland and had no idea what I was in for.

I still recall being in the office in Vancouver trying to formalize my salary with Brian. The idea was that I would receive $10,000 a month to run the show in the province next door. I sat in Brian's office trying to discuss salary and be all businesslike, asking for a contract or something in writing. I vividly recall Brian jumping between three or four tasks as I tried to command his attention. People came in and out of his office asking for a signature here, confirmation of details on a term sheet there, with me interjecting when I could.

He finally looked up at me, then over to his assistant Chantelle, and grunted, "He gets ten." She left the room and came back with a cheque made out to Mike Cameron for $10,000, which he promptly signed. I remembered thinking how unbelievable this all was. It was as if I had just won a scratch-and-win lottery for $10,000. I sat there, holding a cheque that would be my monthly pay for the foreseeable future, an amount that two years earlier I could not have fathomed having in my bank account at any given time. Cheque in hand, I assumed this would be the extent of my written agreement and proceeded to leave the office.

Me? I felt like I was on magic mushrooms, I was Alice in Wonderland chasing a rabbit down the hole and still not entirely sure how I had come to this place Having a six-figure salary and running an office on my own was everything my heart had ever desired, yet I felt like a total sham at the same time, an imposter. I had had no management or leadership training. I was just a naive kid who was quick to follow instructions and who had pushed passed his fear of picking up the phone.

This may have been the first time in my life that I thought about what I now know is called "imposter syndrome." For those of you reading who are true badasses in the business world, you may not be able to relate. You may have earned your keep and worked your way up the ranks, following the natural progression of the expected life cycle of a professional. I had no idea what I was getting into nor what would really be expected of me. At the time, though, it was all rather exhilarating.

Soon after that meeting, I made a trip to Edmonton and met with the property manager for the building we had financed and where my new office would be set up. I arranged for my Porsche to be shipped, had my own office by way of the building we had financed, was no longer in overdraft, and in fact had more money in my bank account than I would have previously thought possible. It's amazing how your perspective can change overnight.

This would have been sometime in August, while my future wife was still off in China and had no knowledge of what was happening in her absence. I returned to Vancouver to await the return of the future Mrs. Cameron, thrilled with the prospect of what lay ahead.

Shortly after her return we found a downtown Edmonton apartment and made the big move. Only after I had been in the Edmonton office for just over a month did I sense that something was a little bit off. The head office was not really giving me direction. I was filling my time with trivial tasks: staying in touch with clients, trying to build new relationships, and meeting as many local connections as I possibly could.

Frank came out to visit during those early days, and I thought we would spend his trip talking strategy and the next steps to building our presence in Northern Alberta. That did not happen. Frank humoured me with the visit, but it was clear that I was nothing more than a distraction to him. I followed him around to a few meetings and made connections with our corporate lawyer in Edmonton, who was more interested in talking about his personal life than in meeting me.

Once again, the scene in the rearview mirror is so much clearer than it was at the time. I recall Frank actively soliciting investors for projects in Eron — projects for which he had money invested.

He was funding himself out.

Such an option had been made an active rule at some point in the previous months. If any of the brokers wanted to get their own money out of projects, they had to "fund them out" themselves, and that was clearly what Frank was doing. He was not raising capital for projects, nor was he raising capital because he believed these were good investments for his clients. He was raising capital to collect his own money — if there was such a thing — before the house of cards came collapsing down around him.

Intellectually, I must have seen all of this playing out before me, but I wanted to believe so badly in the legitimacy of my career opportunity that I ignored the signs. More than signs or even red flags, really, I ignored flashing red alarm bells. Somehow my quest to rack up points on the scorecard overruled my common sense, brain, and intuition.

While it's embarrassing to admit it now, I guess it really wouldn't have mattered at that point. I had relocated myself and my fiancée for the "opportunity" this organization was affording me. I had put my name on the line for Eron's brokerage license with the agency that was in charge of regulating mortgage brokerage activity, the Real Estate Council of Alberta, and really had no other prospects for employment at the time.

I was in far too deep.

WHEN SOMETHING'S GOTTA CHANGE:

It is easy to get bogged down with indecision due to a lack of experience. This can be a massive impediment to personal growth.

What is that thing in your life you know you should be doing but aren't?

____

____

____

____

What would life look like if you used that question as your guide?

____

____

____

____

CHAPTER 13

SHAME

On October 3, 1997, I got *the* phone call. I don't remember exactly who it came from, but it was definitely not from Brian or Frank, my two primary bosses.

As with most Canadian financial services, mortgage brokerage activity is regulated by the government. The agency in the province of British Columbia, where Eron's head office was located, is called The Financial Institutions Commission or FICOM for short. The institution that regulated conduct in the financial securities markets is the BC Securities Commission. The phone call I had received was related to the following release:

Released: October 3, 1997

Contact: Al Clark

Director, Investigations

FICOM, 660-2508

Barbara Barry

660-4800 or (BC only) 1-800-373-6393

Vancouver - The Registrar of Mortgage Brokers has today suspended the registration of Eron Mortgage Corporation under the Mortgage Brokers Act, and frozen related corporate bank accounts.

The Company had offices in Victoria and Vancouver.

The British Columbia Securities Commission has issued a Temporary Cease Trade Order and Notice of Hearing to stop any trading in securities and to prohibit the principals of Eron Mortgage Corporation, Brian Slobogian and Frank Biller, from being directors and officers of any company in B.C.

Allegations which led to the suspension of Eron Mortgage Corporation by the Registrar of Mortgage Brokers include improper transfer of investor funds between investment projects, deficient record keeping, and the raising of funds for non-performing mortgages. In addition, as these companies and individuals are alleged to have been trading in securities without being registered and without receiving a receipt for a prospectus, they were cease traded by the British Columbia Securities Commission.

Investors with questions can telephone a 24 hour toll free number 1-888-555-9299.

Holy shit! This was not something that happened in real life. This was something that happened in a bad "made-for-TV" movie. The ramifications of such a collapse starting to swirl through my head. My clients, my friends, my family?!? All. That. Money. Gone? What would this ultimately mean? I had millions of dollars of people I was close to invested in these projects.

I called FICOM immediately to give them whatever they needed from me. The last thing I wanted was to be on the bad side of a finance regulator. This was one of my first experiences dealing with a regulator of any sort, and I knew my career depended on how I handled this. I felt sick. It took me many attempts to get a hold of them and while I waited, my mind continued to cook up all kinds of stories. Would I be charged? Was I responsible for my investor clients' money? What were the legal, moral and ethical impacts I would have to face?

In hindsight I should have seen their lack of eagerness to talk to me as a good thing. It suggested that they didn't have a whole lot of interest from an enforcement point of view in my involvement. I would later come to know that Eron's demise would turn out to be one of the largest instances of mortgage fraud in the history of the province of British Columbia.

The manager of licensing at The Real Estate Council of Alberta at that time was a fellow by the name of Randy Kilborne. This was where I currently held the Alberta brokerage license on Eron's behalf. I explained to him that Eron had had their license pulled in BC and that I would be withdrawing my license under their banner immediately. I went on to explain that my plan was to stay in Alberta and open my own independent brokerage. I wanted to know if he felt there would be any difficulty if I submitted a licensing application in the future. He indicated that as long as I was not under investigation from the Financial Institutions Commission, there should not be a problem.

I'm not sure how much time actually passed. I did eventually have a conversation with FICOM, the British Columbia regulator, although I was shocked at how little they asked me. I suspected that, given I was one of the earliest employees and on the management team, they might have wanted more. It was quickly apparent that they had very little interest in me. I'm sure there was a part of me that was a bit disappointed: even the regulator didn't think I was enough of a key player to warrant a deeper conversation. But this time, not being one of the "boys" was a good thing.

The weeks following the collapse were a blur. I fielded numerous phone calls from investor clients, many of whom were family, friends, or had been close friends of my family for many years. I want to say that I took all of those calls and that I didn't ignore anyone looking for answers that I simply did not have, but the truth is somewhere in the middle between answering every question and shirking all responsibilities. I didn't run and hide, but there were some phone calls I actively avoided. I was deeply ashamed and embarrassed about what I had let happen to people I genuinely cared about. We were talking about life savings, and in some cases, this money meant the difference between retiring early and not retiring at all.

Even as I write, I can feel the knots in my stomach start to tighten. I was scared and, although I was with my fiancée, I felt alone with a massive weight on my shoulders. I had led those who trusted me, even some whom I loved, into financial ruin, and I was terrified at the prospect of them losing vast amounts of money. It had nothing to do with the quality of investments that I was selling and everything to do with who I was to them. They came because they cared. The shame that I carried with me was immense, a deep sense of regret that would stay with me for a very long time. I was also embarrassed that I had let my quest to become a business rockstar cloud my judgement along the way. If I am being completely honest, I had known that something was not right.

The shame that I carried was immense.

I Should Have Known

It was in the spring prior to the collapse that I decided I had had enough. This is where my memory likely becomes selective to some extent. I had concerns about how the operations were being handled and had discussions with another of the agents in the firm. He had similar concerns, though I cannot tell you if there were specific issues that had raised flags or whether it was simply his gut feeling. The other agent and I discussed breaking away and starting our own firm — at least that was my understanding. I had geared myself up to have the hard conversation with Frank and let him know that I was going to be leaving. Another conflict to which I was not really looking forward.

I had the conversation with Frank, tendering my resignation with the intent of partnering in a new firm. It was only after this that I discovered that the other fellow I was talking to had no intentions of taking on a partner out of the gates and was instead looking for more of a contract employee with some vague suggestion to the potential of partnership in the future. His plan was certainly not what I was expecting and threw me for a bit of a loop.

The next day I received a call from Brian, who wanted me to come down to Vancouver and talk to him about my decision to leave. My head was swimming. I really did not know what to do. I had left the most lucrative job I had ever had, with expectations of partnership that were not reciprocal. When I went to meet Brian, I was as nervous as the very first time I had met him. The sideways glances from the rest of the team in the waiting room where I waited for Brian told me my colleagues knew I had bailed; that knowledge certainly did not help my comfort level. The cold, clammy, sweaty palms were a telltale physical manifestation of how my insides were feeling.

When I was eventually summoned into Brian's office, he presented a much softer, humbler side than I had ever seen before, a complete shock and surprisingly disarming. He asked me to outline my concerns, which I did and which he fully acknowledged. He then went on to explain that much of what I was concerned about, while valid, was simply a function of growing faster than expected. He explained that the recent addition of two senior staff should allay many of my concerns. He had hired a former banking executive as VP of Operations to ensure we had processes in place to deal with the rapid growth, and he had also hired a development expert to assist in the evaluation of new projects, as well as to have the skillset to take over any non-performing projects should they default on their financing.

To this day, I do not know how plausible any of Brian's explanation was or whether it was more a matter of me willing myself to believe.

As Brian concluded his plea for me to reconsider, he sweetened the pot substantially. We had recently brought on a new sales agent with a significant portfolio of investors. He was successfully raising a vast amount of capital for our projects and was an individual I liked and respected. Brian asked if I would consider working under him, assisting with his portfolio. He offered me a base salary, in addition to allowing me to continue to work my own clientele, which amounted to about a $60,000 a year raise with the opportunity to work side by side with someone from whom I believed I could learn a great deal. What I saw as an opportunity at the time I now recognize as a payoff to ignore my gut.

Meanwhile Back In Alberta

This was the lowest point I had ever hit in my life. I was at rock bottom and did not know what to do. Any savings of my own were tied up in "investments" through the company, all of which were now frozen by Price Waterhouse Cooper, the firm appointed as the trustee in charge of affairs. The freeze was in place to see what kind of capital they could recover from any of the projects.

Even as a naive, uneducated young man, I could see the folly of appointing a contractor who was paid exorbitant hourly consulting fees to sift through the ruins. There was absolutely no incentive for these guys to get in, get the job done, and get out. From my point of view, they had a vested interest in dragging the process out as long as possible, since most of any capital recovery went squarely to their top line. Obviously, there was a need for someone to go in and manage the affairs, but it seemed to me that there could have been a much better way of doing business.

But what did I know? The dust would not settle for many, many years, and though I don't know the actual recovery amounts, I would venture a guess that most of the projects returned less than 10 cents on the dollar.

In the end, more than 3,500 investors were bilked out of a total worth of $240 million, a truly obscene amount of money.

Almost eight full years passed before Brian and Frank would face fraud charges. Brian pled guilty to one count of fraud and four counts of theft. He ended up receiving a six-year jail sentence, although I don't know how much time he actually served.

Before Brian went to jail, the *Investor Voice*, an online magazine, painted a bleak picture of him "eeking out a $25,000 per year income as a bookkeeper, his wife working as a sales clerk." They reportedly lived in a $1,000-a-month apartment. It was a far cry from the days when he was stroking out cheques for $20,000 Rolex watches, chartering flights to Vegas, and hiring PGA golf pros to come play at his events. Brian paid an even higher price than prison time when, in 2000, his 21-year-old son died by suicide.

Frank tried to pawn all the blame onto Brian and play the innocent youth. The BC Securities commission issued a ten-year ban on trading of any stock for Frank, although an article from 2012 suggested that he had once again shown up in a Vancouver boiler room, promoting a stock on the over-the-counter bulletin board. The report also indicated that this venture was shut down under suspect terms and that Frank was given a lifetime ban from securities. It would not surprise me in the least to see Frank's name show up in another article somewhere down the road for a similar scenario.

I have seen reports claiming that Frank earned a total of $7 million in commissions over the four-year life of the company. It seems odd to me that someone who had made that kind of money, albeit illegitimately, wouldn't be able to find a way to turn his skills into a legitimate business somehow. I guess this provides some reinforcement for the old adage that a leopard cannot change its spots.

What kind of man has Frank Biller become today? I wonder whether his wife still speaks to him. I wonder if his children are still connected with him and what kind of man they think he is. There was definitely a time in my life where I longed for riches, wealth, and the material possessions that come along with it. Seven million dollars seems like a lot of money, but it's certainly not something for which I would trade my relationship with my kids.

When Intuition Speaks

It is amazing to look back and see how I found ways to justify ignoring my intuition when it didn't align with what I craved intellectually. Do we have to live the mistakes to learn the lessons? Maybe, although I think the better thing to do would be to start practicing paying more attention to our gut.

In my experience, most of us have some level of intuition, though typically we suppress it, deferring to our more rational mind. Intuition is a skill that can be honed with observation and practice. I'm sure you can recall a time in your life that you had a hunch, a feeling, or a gut reaction to a person or a situation in front of you. A time where you ignored that and moved forward anyway, only realizing in hindsight how right you had been.

Many of the practices that I talk about in this book will help you tighten up your intuition. Here are some things you can do on a daily basis to strengthen your connection to your intuition:

1. **Observe:** Practice noticing when your intuition speaks. Notice when your immediate reaction is to squash it.
2. **Ask questions:** Once you notice your intuition speaking to you, start asking it questions. What does this mean? Where is this coming from?
3. **Write it down:** Take a moment to write down what you are feeling and any answers to those questions.
4. **Act!:** Stop ignoring your intuition and begin taking action on it.
5. **Trust the process:** The more we demonstrate faith in our intuition, the more it will start to appear.

I have the good fortune of becoming relatively successful in my chosen profession. Although the path I've taken — leadership over sales — is not the most lucrative that the mortgage industry affords, it's the one that gives me the most satisfaction. My definition of wealth has substantially changed.

And because of Eron, I had learned that satisfaction didn't always look like I thought it would.

WHEN SOMETHING'S GOTTA CHANGE:

It is so easy to shrug off our intuition, to ignore our gut. The reality is that a well-honed sense of intuition can help guide us through life.

The last time intuition was speaking to you, did you listen to it? Why or why not?

____

____

____

____

What were the consequences of listening or not?

____

____

____

____

CHAPTER 14

A NEW LOW

Having lost millions of dollars for friends, family, and clients, this was by far the lowest I had ever felt in my life. Even though the immediate storm had subsided, the dark clouds of despair lingered. The phone calls had slowed when my clients started to realize there was nothing I could do. I had my own demons to wrestle, and without the distraction of trying to assist those whom I had hurt, I was left mired in feelings of guilt, shame, and remorse. At least when I was fielding phone calls, it felt like I was making some kind of contribution. I was able to numb myself from the internal angst through the distraction of keeping busy.

I skirted the edges of depression as I kept trying to move forward, and I had no one to whom I could turn. My parents had bailed me out enough in the past, and now I had cost them a substantial amount of their retirement savings. I did not yet have the relationship skills to "turn towards" my fiancée, as Dr. John Gottman so eloquently describes as one of the nine components of the "Sound Relationship House." I once again felt like an imposter and a complete failure of a human being. Had I a better understanding of what it might look like to explore and share my true feelings, I might have moved through these difficult emotions with more clarity and a greater ability to extract the lessons being presented. Instead, while fully aware of the circumstances, I did not grasp the magnitude of the emotions that accompanied them.

I. Went. Numb.

What little experience I had in the business world had turned out to be a complete sham. I had been successful, but the experience wasn't exactly something I could proudly post on my resumé for my next potential employer to peruse.

After the harsh reality of what had happened sank in, I started to try and answer that elusive question: what now?

I remember discussing possibilities with Christine, my fiancée at the time, and weighing our options. It didn't seem like many were available. The decision really seemed to be about whether or not to stay in Edmonton and start over, or to go back to Vancouver and start over again. When we started to mentally build our pros and cons lists, there wasn't a lot of debate required. We could go back to Vancouver, where my name would be attached to the largest fraud scheme in BC history, or we could stay and roll the dice in a new town that would not have Eron Mortgage plastered all over the front pages of the newspapers.

Ultimately, the choice was easy. We had no firm ties anywhere yet — no real estate, no children, no jobs, school, or anything connecting us to any geographic location. In 1997, the Alberta Advantage was just starting to get underway. The economy was strong and growing, and opportunity seemed abundant. We agreed on what I would later recall as our five-year plan. We'd give it a try and see how we fared in

Edmonton. (At this point, I think I am somewhere around year 20 of that five-year plan.)

I decided that I would set up shop as an independent mortgage broker. I had been recently introduced to the concept of brokering residential mortgages for major banks and lending institutions. Oddly, it was a concept I had never considered. My only exposure to real estate financing had been what I had learned at Eron — dealing with private investment capital for large syndicated mortgages. Lending bank money to regular folk for traditional home mortgages seemed like an insanely easy way to make a living, and I was extremely excited.

If the possibilities weren't attractive enough, I found out there was also software that could directly connect me to a number of major lending institutions. All I had to do was get my customers' application data into the system, and I could send it directly to any number of lenders for their consideration and, hopefully, a mortgage commitment. Not only could I send this data electronically, but if the lender accepted the application, they would pay me a fee for sending them the business.

Almost everyone at some point in their lives would need a mortgage in order to buy a home. This would be like shooting fish in a barrel, I reasoned.

The ominous shadow of despair that had fallen on me in the wake of the Eron debacle started to lift. The clouds began to part, and the first rays of sunlight poked through. Eager to learn from the mistakes I had made so far, I started thinking of what I was going to call my next foray into the business world. My quest to wield the moniker "badass businessman" was not yet vanquished.

I laugh now when I recount how naive I was. Clearly, I still had lessons to learn.

I started toying with name ideas and landed on the name Alta

Mortgage and Investments. Keeping "investment" in the name was important to me because I still truly believed in the possible advantages that mortgages as an investment provided. The difference this time would be proper, ethical execution that would legitimately work for investors. I had seen it done at the garden supply store, where their pension plan had been invested in private mortgages, working rather well for them.

With a corporate name registered, a plan in place, and a fire in my heart, I was ready to make this the best five-year plan anyone had ever seen.

Unfortunately, the universe had other plans and fate was not done with me yet.

Liar, Liar Affidavits On Fire

In November of 1997, I put together all the requisite licensing forms to apply for my corporate brokerage license. I needed to apply for both a corporate brokerage license as well as an individual agent's license. I would be the "designated agent" for the brokerage. Once the licensing was in place, I could be on my way to financial independence, becoming a titan of industry in the mortgage brokering world like none before me.

I was a little nervous about this venture, given my past experiences in British Columbia. Since I had discussed the matter with the manager of licensing just a few short weeks earlier and he had seemed comfortable with the idea, I assured myself I was overreacting. I had never been charged, convicted, or even investigated by any regulatory authorities at all. In fact, as I mentioned before, I was so far off their radar I was almost insulted. With the paperwork submitted, all I could do was get as much of my marketing plan ready while I awaited licensing approval.

But the approval never came. Instead, I received a phone call from Mr. Kilborne informing me that I had sworn a false affidavit, a very serious, and possibly criminal, offense. My application was denied pending an investigation into the matter.

I was absolutely stunned. I had my concerns that Eron might come back to haunt me, but the accusation of my swearing a false affidavit made no sense at all. So much for the light at the end of the Eron tunnel. Suddenly, that tunnel seemed to get a whole lot longer than I expected.

It turned out that in the application they had posed five questions, beginning with:

1. Have you ever been bankrupt? *No*
2. Have you ever been convicted of a criminal offense? *No*
3. Have you ever had your license suspended or revoked? *No*

According to the Real Estate Council of Alberta, my answer to number three was wrong. Since Eron had had *its* brokerage license revoked, I therefore had had *my* sub mortgage broker's license revoked.

When I realized what had happened and where the misunderstanding was, I was actually quite relieved. *Okay*, I thought, *this is an easy fix. I can just explain that I had never personally been a part of any disciplinary proceedings, and we'll be good to go.*

Wrong!

I continued to explain that I had not knowingly sworn a false affidavit, because I had not realized that my license had been revoked along with Eron's. I had spoken to the manager of licensing the very day Eron had its license revoked — so quickly, in fact, that *I* was the one who had broken the news to *him*.

Unfortunately, my case had already been referred for investigation, and that investigation would take place no matter what the explanation was for the error.

I accepted my fate, but just how long would I have to wait?

Up to six months, they said.

What the hell am I supposed to do to feed my family in the meantime?

I was quickly knocked back into despair but set out to find a solution.

Back To Work

I recalled a conversation with our landlord, a self-employed cribber, a concrete worker who had more business than he knew what to do with. Aaron and I had become friends over the few months Christine and I had been renting from him, so I called him up and asked if he would consider letting me work for him to pay rent while we waited for this licensing disaster to pass.

He found it extremely amusing that this white-collar, wannabe broker was having to resort to blue-collar labour to make ends meet. I thought it would be fun to learn the other side of the business. I had, after all, helped finance many homes, businesses, and commercial projects in my career. Why not learn the construction side as well? And I was no stranger to manual labour after my days in Australia and Greenleaf Garden Supplies.

My landlord was generous in allowing me to work with him, even though I had absolutely zero construction experience. As it turned out, I also had less than zero aptitude for construction.

It wasn't exactly the best time of year for me to start my foray into the trades. It was the middle of winter in Northern Alberta, and we were mostly working on foundations. Absolutely everything we did was outside. As I recall, the process was dependent on several factors. Obviously, each style of house called for something different, and depending on structural requirements, we were sometimes required to pour piles of varying depths on which the footing would lay. We would frame and pour the footing based on specs, and these would become the base for the foundation walls.

My favourite part of the job was returning to remove the forms after the concrete had set. To break the snap ties that held the forms together meant slinging a hammer, something I found extremely satisfying. It was almost like unwrapping a present. We had worked hard to build the forms and pour the concrete, and we'd soon see the fruits of our labour standing strong and tall, ready to support an entire house that was yet to be built.

There was immense satisfaction in standing on the street curb in a subdivision under construction, looking at the beginning of someone's future dream home. I vividly recall the sounds of other tradespeople working on houses at various stages of construction, the smell of dirt and freshly poured concrete, the odd whiff of diesel in the air, and the incessant beeping of a truck backing into another lot. I probably take more satisfaction now in the memory than I did at the time. But even then, knowing that memories would be made on the basis of something I built with my own two hands was a different kind of feeling than financing a project. It was a new experience, and I was surprised at how uplifting it felt.

Framing the forms at odd angles made some parts of the job challenging. I remember one particular time when, after hitting my thumb with a hammer and cursing my ineptitude out loud, I looked over to find my landlord leaning over a shovel watching me from across the lot. His eyes smiled as he caught my gaze, and he called out, "Hey, Broker! How you doing over there?" It was the kind of compassionate mocking that only a few can pull off.

While I thoroughly enjoyed my brief stint in the trades, I was eager to get back behind a desk where I belonged. This experience gave me a much greater appreciation for the things I did well...and those that I did not. I learned a lot about what it took to build a house — and that I really had no interest in doing it anymore. All I could do was hope that my broker's license would come through sooner rather than later.

I had decided that I would bend over backwards from the outset to play nice and assist where I could with the investigation. When I finally received an opportunity to be interviewed by the investigator, I was excited, because it meant actual progress was being made. We had a good conversation, and I felt my story was well received. As I often do after a new business introduction, whether they are investigating me or not, I sent a follow-up thank you card. I always endeavour to make a strong and lasting impression on anyone I meet and figured that this might be even more important with the regulator's investigator.

This polite gesture was apparently a very bad idea.

The manager of licensing at RECA called, not to inform me that a decision had been made about my fate, but to tell me that sending their investigator a thank you card was inappropriate and seen as trying to unduly influence the investigator.

Fortunately, it only took four months for my little licensing investigation to come to a resolution. I really struggled with how long it took and, in my view, how asinine the entire process was.

In the end, they denied my request for a brokerage license.

Once again, I was at a crossroads.

WHEN SOMETHING'S GOTTA CHANGE:

When things do not go our way, we have choices. We can get down and out or we can get busy.

How do negative events in your life impact the quality of your relationships?

____

____

____

____

When things go sideways, do you turn towards the people you love?

____

____

____

____

CHAPTER 15

MY BABIES AND ME

After several months of back and forth, the Alberta Regulator would allow me to register as an agent under a brokerage that was a member in good standing with the Alberta Mortgage Brokers Association. While I was a little bit disappointed, I was not entirely surprised. The decision still gave me the opportunity to become a licensed broker and earn a living in the profession that I had chosen.

It was time for me to keep it simple. No more high flying, high risk, high reward type brokering. I would be extremely happy to settle into a role as a residential "A" mortgage broker in a place where I could legitimately assist homeowners with their dreams by placing their financing for them. I set out to find a brokerage that I liked and that would consider taking me on. I grabbed a Yellow Pages — yes, the actual Yellow Pages book — and started calling around to some of the brokerages in the area.

I remember my first meeting with a brokerage well. I recall the owner simply asking me how much business I had at the moment. After learning I had never written a residential mortgage in my life, he asked me if I had enough savings in the bank to carry my sorry ass for the next six months. I lied and told him I did. We shook hands and parted ways.

This was my first real lesson in the cold, hard reality of the residential mortgage business. I had expected that my stature as a bigtime businessman would garner me a little more cachet, but this was clearly one-sided thinking.

Another expert recommended that I get a brand name behind me to give me a little more credibility in the residential space. I could do this by working for a bank as a mortgage specialist. I took this advice.

Soon, I was offered a job with CIBC Mortgages for a fully commissioned position and with the benefits associated with working for a large financial institution. They provided me with training that included flying me out to Toronto for an 11-day course covering all the bases. They introduced me to the business of placing residential mortgages through one of the largest financial institutions in the country. Although I wasn't brokering, I was selling one line of products for a single financial institution, and I soon recognized this fabulous training ground would eventually lead me back to independent brokering. I worked hard and soon got the hang of the business.

Getting Schooled

Always one to seek opportunity for growth, I set a goal of getting my business diploma with a specialization in real estate. I found a four-year distance education diploma that I could complete via correspondence. The Urban Land Economics program was offered through the University of British Columbia. I went online to register and began the application process, excited about the prospect of becoming a university graduate after being such a disappointment in high school.

That's when it happened, the one requirement I had not even thought to anticipate:

"PLEASE SEND US YOUR HIGH SCHOOL TRANSCRIPT."

I sat there staring at the screen for a minute, feeling utterly defeated. Maybe I shouldn't have cared so much. I was doing well selling mortgages for the bank and made a comfortable living for us, yet I still felt a nagging sense of underachievement. Ready to shut my browser and call it a day, my eyes scanned down the page to see the next line of text:

"...OR ENTER YOUR UBC STUDENT NUMBER."

I had received a University of British Columbia student number when I had enrolled in my mortgage brokers licensing course but wasn't sure what would happen if I entered it. I slowly keyed in the student number, finished the form, and hit submit.

"APPLICATION ACCEPTED. YOU WILL HEAR FROM US SHORTLY."

My heart raced with a mix of excitement, disbelief, and wonder. For the next three weeks, life was even more exciting as I checked the mailbox daily in anticipation.

I was still a little stunned when my enrollment package, including course material and assignment sheets, was delivered.

This high school dropout was now officially a university student.

Things were looking up. Business was progressing, I was soon to be a university graduate, and family life was kicking into high gear. In October of 2000, I was well on my way to achieving domestic bliss when we were blessed with our first child, a bouncing baby boy. When I say "bouncing," I mean literally. This one had a surplus of energy only surpassed by his wilful stubbornness. I honestly don't know where he got that from, though if you ask my parents, they might have some ideas.

Payback is a bitch.

I remember purchasing an expensive glider chair for his room. We had visions of our sweet little baby boy snuggled on our laps while we read him stories and gently rocked the little angel to sleep. That might have been the case for a little while, but I don't honestly remember, because those initial years were a bit of a blur. Chris did not sleep much at all, and as a result neither did we. By the time he learned to crawl, he was doing laps around our precious gliding chair. We continued to read to him every night, albeit not exactly as we had envisioned, and he was still our precious little gift.

I secretly admired his spunk, defiance, and inner rebel, but I can assure you that it was definitely a secret. If you're a parent, you understand those years were precious but not an easy time.

In December of 2002, we welcomed our second child, a baby girl. How perfect was that? I now had the million-dollar family: beautiful wife, two healthy kids (one girl, one boy) —my dream come true without any shadow of a doubt.

I'm not entirely sure where the time went, but it did. We moved from diapers to toilet training, from crawling to toddling, then to walking upright like real little human beings. I have to admit, it was a pretty amazing metamorphosis to watch.

As my kids were growing, so was I. With strong mentorship by my sales manager Merv, I prospered. I was given an office in one of the local real estate offices, where I built on my skills cultivating and building relationships and continued to prospect for business. I found an easy aptitude for the business and really enjoyed assisting people, especially young families, with their objective of obtaining home ownership. While I was never in the top ten at CIBC across the country, I was always in the top 50 nationally. The bank provided me with excellent opportunity to grow as a mortgage salesperson, giving me both exceptional training and incentives.

But I knew at some point I would end up back in the world of brokering. The idea of being able to arrange financing for clients at a number of different financial institutions based on their needs had tremendous appeal to me.

Eventually, CIBC also provided us with the opportunity to place mortgages with various lenders outside the bank's group of companies. We would be allowed to broker our clients' mortgages in the event that they did not fit within the CIBC portfolio. We eventually rebranded from CIBC Mortgages to Home Loans Canada or HLC Mortgages.

This worked well for a while, becoming problematic only when I started finding more favourable mortgage solutions for my clients at some of these alternate lenders. Many of the products these other lenders offered were simply superior for the client, and I was not about to start promoting products that were less than optimal just because of the company brand. After several divergences of opinion and multiple slaps on my wrist, I made plans to leave the bank to set up my own mortgage brokerage.

I needed to do things my way, and that meant integrity had to come first. Thus, on December 23, 2003, my third child, Integrity First Mortgage Solutions Inc., was born.

WHEN SOMETHING'S GOTTA CHANGE:

Growth and evolution are concepts that need to be intentionally cultivated. We can place stepping stones along the path of our lives. The lesson here is really to focus on consciously creating and stepping into our future selves.

Where can you find opportunities for growth in your life?

____

____

____

____

What can you do right now to foster the evolution of who you are?

____

____

____

____

CHAPTER 16

CREATIVITY

Integrity First Mortgage Solutions began with a $5,000 cash injection, an early inheritance gift from my parents when they sold their home in Vancouver. I excelled as a "solopreneur" and soon realized that in order to grow, I needed to move out of the basement office in the house Christine and I owned and get into a real office environment. I rented a small 750 sq. foot office and hired my first assistant. Business was great and I had big plans. Eventually a number of my former colleagues at HLC Mortgages started to inquire about what I was doing and what my plans were. Within that first year of operation, five of them followed me and came to work for my fledgling brokerage. Over the next three years, we continued to grow and solidify as an organization, becoming a well-respected independent brokerage.

In the mortgage industry, as brokers we're paid a finder's fee based on the dollar amount of the transaction that we originate. On top of that amount, there is additional compensation known as the volume bonus, and yes, it is exactly what you would expect it to be:

lenders compensate organizations at different levels based on their overall corporate volumes. These volume bonuses were meant as an incentive for the brokerage head office to encourage their agents to use a certain lender.

The challenge this presented to a smaller, independent brokerage — one originating somewhere in the neighbourhood of $200 million in annual mortgage volume — was that it made it hard for a small company like Integrity First to be competitive with the national super brokers. These brokerages were originating in excess of $5 billion in annual volume and were earning larger point percentages because of their volume. If we as a smaller company wanted maximum compensation for our brokers, we would need to narrow our lender pool, potentially limiting choice for our consumer, something we did not feel was ethically right.

This presented a real conundrum for the brokerage. Our options were limited. The most logical solution was to join an existing super broker, which meant we'd have to pay a portion of our compensation to the house for the privilege of being associated with them. While financially this option might have made sense, my independent spirit rebelled. The whole premise of the volume bonus was starting to bother me more and more. Something just did not seem right. If you're thinking it might be time to cue the crusade music, you'd be right.

Sometimes in business we have to find creative solutions to common problems.

In 2006, a competitor launched. Their value proposition was to entice the independent brokerages by promising the continuance of independence, while also allowing pooled access to aggregate volume bonus at a small royalty fee of 5%. It was a brilliant concept. The founder, based on existing relationships with lender partners, was able to negotiate the grandfathering of volume bonus payments with the promise of volume targets yet to come. I did not understand how big a feat this was at the time.

In case that sounds confusing, let me give you this example. If ten different brokerages were each giving a lender $10 million in volume, that lender was getting a total of $100 million in volume. If the lender's threshold for volume bonus was $100 million, they were currently paying no or minimal volume bonus to these ten firms who individually weren't making the cut. However, if these same ten firms all pooled under this new aggregator, their $10 million each would combine to create $100 million in volume, and they were now eligible for additional compensation. There was no additional value added to this volume for the lenders. It simply cost them more today for the same volume they were getting yesterday.

I'm not sure why those policy decisions were made or who made them, but this clearly demonstrates the great value of relationship. This was most certainly a relationship decision, not a prudent business one for our lender partners.

From the perspective of the smaller brokerage, joining the new aggregator on the scene really made a lot of economic sense. In theory, you could maintain your own independent brand, pay a 5% royalty fee, and in many cases see as much as a 25% increase in revenue thanks to qualifying for the volume bonus as part of the group. In other words, these broker owners could pay a nickel to receive a quarter.

For me, however, it was much more about a sense of righteous indignation than it was about any monetary implications. It frustrated me to no end that a brokerage down the street from me — doing less than a tenth of the volume I did — could now join this new organization, pay a 5% royalty fee, and immediately be paid more by my lender partners than I would. I found it staggering that our lender partners would play along with this system. They were empowering one individual to profit by aggregating volume that they already had, therefore costing themselves more money in the end. There was no logical explanation for the lenders' complicity, and the practice would prove to be the beginning of the end of volume bonuses as we knew them.

One weekend, because I had been one of the co-creators of an affordable housing initiative we called the HOME Program, I was invited to speak at an affordable housing conference taking place in Jasper, Alberta. It was on the four-hour drive out to Jasper, with "Pretty Vegas" by INXS blasting on repeat, that the simple solution to my righteous anger occurred to me: I would form a non-profit cooperative that would allow the smaller independents to aggregate volume strictly for the purpose of volume bonus. We'd band together to make this thing fair.

I set to work implementing the idea of the cooperative entity, a great personal exercise in organization building and thinking things out well in advance. From financing to governance, I would have to come up with a model that would work for everyone involved. I contacted a lawyer friend of mine whom I had met through Toastmasters. I explained what I was hoping to accomplish and discussed governance and other issues with him. We incorporated as a non-profit corporation, and I set to work.

The pitch to other brokerages was relatively easy, and as soon as I articulated my vision, most of the broker owners to whom I spoke understood it immediately. I started asking my lending partners and other industry peers who else might be a candidate to join the movement. After all, that was really what this was about, creating a movement, a national alliance of independent brokers. We all shared a similar challenge, and for the most part we were all looking for the same thing.

The objective here was quite simple: to level the playing field for the independent broker owner and to remove the need to join a national super broker.

I cold-called many of the major independents in the province and across the country. I was still an unknown commodity in the broker community nationally and had not really earned my stripes, so to speak. Over and over, broker owners I contacted listened to my story and, while cool to a sales pitch initially, started to warm as the idea unfolded. I could feel the understanding growing. I called one particular broker in Calgary who had been referred to me. He listened intently and then did the verbal equivalent of a shrug and suggested I call another broker who, in his words, "was always up for a good crusade."

I made the call and the individual listened, understood, and immediately saw the opportunity. A few days, and many phone calls later, that broker and I had rounded up a strong group of reputable Calgary brokers. I arranged to make a trip down to Calgary and attend a presentation on the concept to this group. Unfortunately, when I got there, I realized this individual had decided to take the idea and try and monetize it, the complete opposite of my altruistic vision. I left the meeting feeling more than a little dejected and frustrated that I had not achieved what I was hoping to accomplish. In fact, this individual formed a new organization that would essentially compete with what I was trying to set up.

Eventually I incorporated under Part II of the Canada Corporations Act as a non-profit named The National Alliance of Independent Mortgage Brokers. We had eleven brokerages that agreed to be a part of this newly-formed organization and our governance structure included representation from across the country. We agreed to hold monthly teleconference meetings to move forward our agenda. We were each a part of *something*!

The only challenge I faced was that I really only had leverage with the one or two lenders with whom I did a significant amount of volume. The good news? The competing organization that was born from our Calgary meeting put pressure on the one lender on whom they had leverage, thus setting a precedent that I could tap into. The other organization was short lived and never really materialized. In contrast, I covered all the start-up and ongoing costs of the organization initially and ended up charging our eleven members an annual fee of $1500. I chaired the organization as a volunteer, and we ran like that for about 18 months. It was a great start to a fantastic idea. While we had some traction with both lenders and brokers, our growth flattened, and it soon became evident that we would need more than volunteer leadership to accomplish our goals.

Around the time that our growth was tapering off, I received a phone call from one of our members, Gord Ross, who expressed some of these same concerns. He informed me that he had looked at all of the available competing brokerage models and had decided he needed to join one of them. We discussed what he wanted to do, and he went on to list all the things he was going to do after joining the other organization.

I said, "Isn't it ridiculous that you are going to join one of these organizations, pay a bunch of money in royalty fees, and still have to come up with much of what you need on your own?"

Gord replied, "There is just no one doing it right."

"Why don't we do it right then?"

"What do you mean?"

"Let's get together and figure out what needs to exist and create it," I replied.

We hashed out a plan to evolve our non-profit into a for-profit model by increasing the fees charged and providing additional value by way of a technology platform. That would be the origin story for Axiom Mortgage Partners, a national network of independently owned and operated brokerages.

Fuelled by passion and purpose — to level the playing field for the independent broker owner — we prospered.

As time went on and we continued to grow, I started getting invited to participate in larger-scale industry meetings. I was sitting at the big boys' table.

Talk about the imposter syndrome kicking in. Mine was in full swing, likely the reason we ended up stagnating at times. Self-doubt will kill you every time. While I truly believed I was on the right path and my motives were completely altruistic, something in my mind still said, "You don't deserve to be here."

I don't know why. When I look at the individuals who have accomplished great things in this world, I wonder why I believe they are any more talented, smarter, or luckier than I am. People with less talent, fewer skills, or poorer work ethics would do things that I wanted to do, and only later did I realize the only thing holding me back was...me.

The feelings of unworthiness that prevent you from moving ahead as quickly as you should aren't always overt emotions that you can identify. In fact, they're usually far more insidious and tend to sneak up on you. You find yourself procrastinating about things you know you should be doing, even though delaying these things will bring sure ruin to anything you have ever built.

Confidence is a fickle thing. You may feel like you have it. You may even have it intellectually and emotionally, and all the behaviour that goes with it, but there are still remnants of unworthiness that linger and force you to perform at a lower level of which you are capable . Defeating that insidious voice is sometimes a daily fight but one that's well worth it.

As I reflect on the journey to create the cooperative and eventually the national network, it strikes me how much of an impact we have had on the industry. Gord and I ran the network together but continued to manage our own smaller brokerages separately as licensees under the network. In 2008 we decided that there was no point in maintaining two unique brokerages, so Unisource Mortgage and Integrity First Mortgage Solutions merged to become Axiom Mortgage Solutions.

We certainly missed opportunities, had some big wins, experienced bitter disappointments, and dropped several balls along the way, but the truth of the matter is we made history, a history that few know. I was passionate about the work we were doing and threw myself into it full tilt. I was successful by all accounts, and I was making an impact in an industry I loved.

Little did I know the price I would have to pay for this success on the family front.

It took me a long time to realize that I was following someone else's playbook — and that my kids were not seeing me live the kind of life I wanted them to have as a model.

Their dad? I was playing society's game and was about to be heavily penalized.

WHEN SOMETHING'S GOTTA CHANGE:

Looking back on what we created, I realize how boldly creative I had to be to conceptualize what was ultimately built. For a very long time I would have insisted I do not have a creative bone in my body. I now realize how ridiculous this sentiment is. I also realize how much that might have held me back.

What would your life look like if you embraced your creativity, whatever that looks like?

____

____

____

____

In what areas of your life can you look for creative solutions to problems you see there?

____

____

____

____

CHAPTER 17

FALLING OUT OF LOVE

From the outside looking in, we must have looked like the picture-perfect family. Christine and I made the conscious choice to have her stay home and raise our children while I went to work at CIBC and then went on to create Integrity First Mortgage Solutions in order to provide financially for our family. She took the kids to school and ran the household, which gave me an extraordinary ability to build my business. I worked long hours and made a relatively good living for us.

I am extremely grateful that we had the ability to make this choice for our family. I will forever be happy for the bond that this helped my children form with their mother and for the opportunity this gave us to raise our kids in a manner that allowed them to see our values. In this world where we are bombarded with marketing messages from brands trying to shape our values and control our pocketbook, instilling solid core values in the little ones we raise is more important than ever. Values become our baseline for the decisions we make.

When we talk of gender equality these days, we typically talk about the role of women in the workplace, about equal wages for equal work, and about the disproportionate balances of power in companies and corporations globally — very real issues. While I think there has been a lot of movement to allow for work equality, in the context of roles within the family, I'm not sure the home front has seen the same improvements. I still love the idea of traditional family values, but that thinking really segregates the roles. If you're not careful, it can cause a great divide between you and your spouse.

We were not careful.

Christine continued to fall deeper into the role of mother, and I continued to fall deeper into the role of provider. She had her way of rearing our children, and unfortunately, my ways of doing things were often quite different, even though our values aligned. This ended up causing significant conflict and resentment between the two of us. I suspect this tale is played out fairly often in my generation.

Once, when our children were still very young, we attended a family wedding. We sat with my Aunt Sharon, who talked to us about the importance of putting our relationship as a couple first. She counselled that, in addition to attending to the children's needs, we needed to guard our relationship and ensure that the two of us nurtured our relationship and watered the seeds of romance within our marriage. We left the wedding and continued that conversation in private.

We didn't agree on the priority of our relationship over the children. We had vastly differing opinions, and I knew at that moment those differences would become a problem. I'm not suggesting the fault was with my wife; I certainly could have made more effort in our relationship over the course of the years to ensure that she *wanted* me to be a priority. I am a salesman, after all. Clearly, I did not do a good job in this regard.

As time passed, I felt more and more like an observer in the lives of my wife and children. I still went to all of their events and was almost always there at bedtime. I coached soccer, attended performances, drove to dance and music and all the myriad of activities that they did. Yet somehow, I was still an outsider. But that was okay, I told myself. I was working hard and providing for my family. I had worked my whole life for this role — building a good life for our family and working hard to afford us some privilege. We had a nice house with a double car garage and two vehicles. We took a tropical winter vacation every year and made an annual pilgrimage to visit my parents in their beachfront house in the Fraser Valley in British Columbia. Was this not everything the perfect family man could ever dream of?

A distant marriage and an outsider relationship with my kids? The narrative was not the one I would have written for my life, not even close.

Early in 2012, while I was alone in Jamaica on a reward trip with one of our lending partners, I had one of the most pivotal moments of my life. I was staying at a five-star resort right on the beach and with every possible comfort seen to by the butler assigned to our room.

I was in paradise, yet there was something missing.

On the exterior, in that moment my life was amazing.

I was sitting, book in hand, on a lounge chair by the pool, overlooking the ocean and an absolutely stunning beach. I took the drink I had just been brought, thanked the server, put the book down, and drank in the experience. The sun shone, the breeze blew, and the sound of waves crashed on the beach.

I was in paradise, yet there was something missing.

Then I saw them, a couple in their mid-sixties walking along the water's edge, hand in hand, simply enjoying each other. They looked so content, the epitome of what I wanted for my retirement life: to spend my time hand in hand with the woman I loved.

Time stood still as the possibility of a new reality unfolded before me. In that moment, I knew that the current state of my marriage was never going to provide that. Something needed to change. I had let over a decade go by and had fallen into complacency, blindly accepting a reality that was not what I wanted. It was time for me to take action. It was time for me to take responsibility for my life and, since I could not accept it, to change it.

Ever the pragmatist, I started to look at what my options actually were: I could leave and consider a life as a divorced man, or I could make some effort to reconcile and see if we could get back to a point where we might end up as that elderly couple walking the beach hand in hand. I had invested 15 years in this relationship with a woman whom I had loved dearly at some point in time. Throwing that all away was not my first choice.

Since I am the one telling this story, I would love to tell you that I wanted desperately to make things work, that I put aside my selfish desires and did what I could to save my fading marriage. This is certainly the person I would like to have been, but the reality was, I instead went through the motions, checking all the boxes you are supposed to check when trying to salvage a marriage.

After I returned from the Caribbean, I had a conversation with Christine and suggested that we go to counselling to see if "we could make it work." Since I am being honest, my "effort" was a sham. By the time I returned home from that Jamaica trip, and in spite of multiple sessions of marriage counselling that would follow, I was realizing that, despite my upbringing and strong sense of family, my marriage was not the right thing for me.

I can't recall the exact words spoken in our final therapy session, but I can certainly tell you the sentiment. When I walked into that meeting, my heart was cold. The way I was feeling, there was no option for a positive outcome. I wasn't even sure why I was there. I had shut down.

In that final meeting, our counsellor asked us questions about feelings, and I'm sure it very quickly became apparent to Christine that I was in a place where I could not see any resolution to the conflicts we were facing. After a few failed attempts to bring me back to a place of emotional engagement, the therapist finally opted for a different strategy. She looked at my wife and said, "I'd like to talk to each of you individually."

Christine left the room and the therapist spoke directly to me. After a few short minutes of trying to break through my armour-plated heart, our therapist resigned herself to the new reality of where we were in this conversation. She subsequently asked me to wait in a room a few doors down. She brought Christine back into the therapy room, and I sat alone.

My heart was stone, my mind numbed in a dispassionate denial of what my life had become. I heard a spine-tingling wail from down the hall as the therapist brought my wife into the new reality of the world in which we were now living.

When the therapist eventually brought us back together, the energy shift was palpable. A heaviness blanketed the entire room and likely extended beyond the walls of that small office. The language immediately changed from reconciliation to mediation: "Sometimes, despite best efforts for reconciliation...."

My mind began racing. This was really happening. It felt very much like I was in a dissociative state, observing the goings on of someone who was not me. Then I was abruptly yanked back to the moment at hand.

"Mike," the therapist began, "I have discussed this with Christine, and I think that you should take some of your things and move out of the house this afternoon." Obviously, this was a very logical conclusion to the events that had led up to this moment, but I'm not sure I had gotten that far in my mind. The mechanics of this realization finally took a hold of me.

Where would I go?

What would we tell the kids?

What the fuck had I just done?

I'm lucky. Today, my kids are happy and healthy teens, able to enjoy each other's company and share video games. What more could a dad want? They both make me extremely proud and have for their own brands of individual greatness. Christopher is a smart, kind, and gentle soul with a lot of compassion; Mikaela is hard working, creative, and wise beyond her years. I am excited and have tremendous hopes for them and the future world in which they will grow up, live, and eventually make their own mark. But my greatest hope is that they'll determine early what kind of people they want to become and focus on *becoming* in their own way.

Since I have the luxury of painting the canvas with the brush of my choosing, I may have acquired a skewed image of the reality of who I was then, but my hope is to allow you to see it from my perspective so that you may learn from my mistakes, just as I eventually would.

I had done other things over the years that contributed to the collapse of our marriage. I am not proud of everything I have done, and I take nothing less than full responsibility for what happened between us. Perhaps my story will serve as a cautionary tale for you and your significant other. Perhaps if I had been a stronger man back then, if I had had the courage to truly show up and be seen in our marriage, the results would have been different. Maybe if I could have been just a little more present

Perhaps my story will serve as a cautionary tale.

and connected, I would not be where I was this day. And maybe if I had made different decisions along the way, Christine and I might have salvaged the love we once had for each other. I really don't know.

What I do know is that this is another time where I ignored the warning signs along the way. Much like what happened in the Eron Mortgage fiasco, I had become wilfully blind to the signs, omens, portents, or whatever you want to call them that life presented to me. There are many moments within our marriage that should have served as markers for both of us to make changes. The conversation on our priorities — our children versus our relationship — was a warning that I chose to ignore. I should have recognized this subject as a speed bump, a hurdle, perhaps even a fork in the road. With my tendency to avoid conflict, I took the easy path. When we take the easy path to avoid the small conflicts, we simply defer the conflict and allow it to fester and build. Ultimately, for me, that reached an unresolvable breaking point. I had allowed this to go on for much longer than it should have.

Maybe it was the serene setting of the tropics that finally allowed awareness to come out of my periphery and into the centre of my focal point. Whatever it was, it was my first step. Once again, I am reminded that the first step to change is awareness. It was in that moment of realization that I made a decision. I made a decision and I was going to do something about it. I decided that something had to change, and it was on me to make that happen.

Warning signs are as important to recognize in your relationships as they are everywhere else in your life. The first step in making change is awareness. You have to recognize those little signposts that are presented to you. You also have to accept them for what they are, without shame or judgement.

Despite my awareness that my marriage was no longer working, I did not move to the acceptance part. Had I made the conscious choice at the time to either accept or reject the status quo, I could have acted on it rather than let it mushroom into the untenable situation in which I eventually found myself.

After that last counselling session, I was simultaneously relieved that this chapter of turmoil was coming to an end yet terrified at the prospect of what the future held.

That future quickly arrived on a half-inflated air mattress.

The next morning, I woke in a fuzzy, shock-induced haze in my brother's spare room less than 24 hours past the last-ditch effort to save my doomed marriage. A hurriedly packed duffle bag sat on the floor beside me, a $27 portable oscillating fan tilted back and forth, blowing the winds of change my way. My pillow, spare sheets, and a bottle of water were the extent of the comforts of home surrounding me.

Except I wasn't at home. I was light years away from anything I could have imagined.

My wife and I were separated, and I was alone.

While I may not be proud of every twist and turn I have taken on this journey, I am damn proud of who I am today. I am equally proud to strive to become the better man — father, friend, partner — that I know lies deep within me, the man whose soul is in the process of awakening.

I can assure you, though, that there is very little in this life that I would change. Everything that has happened, has happened to make me into the man that I am. I have fully created this perfectly imperfect, flawed, and always striving individual I am today.

Without each and every unique, pleasant, horrifying, and otherwise painful experience, I would not be the person I am today.

WHEN SOMETHING'S GOTTA CHANGE:

Sometimes life does not unfold the way we think it is supposed to. Sometimes, this is not a bad thing.

How have your dreams changed over the years with the challenges that arose?

____

____

____

____

What changing circumstances do you still need to make your peace with?

____

____

____

____

CHAPTER 18

SUCCESS TO SIGNIFICANCE

If you've ever tried going out on your own, you know that the grand idea of entrepreneurship and the tough reality of running a business are very different. In fact, I'll admit that being the successful entrepreneur with plenty of cash to blow and all the trappings of a big-shot businessman was everything of which I had ever dreamed. Until, that is, I actually went out there and did it on my own. After over a decade of being a successful entrepreneur, I started to realize that material success, once you have it, isn't all it's cracked up to be.

In those first few years of being single, I spent a lot of time not trying to *become* more but to really step into and own who I already was. For years, I had chased the idea of material success. Now, in my 40s and finally happy in my life, striving to be my true self, my idea of success was evolving along with my idea of who I was. My brokerage was successful on paper and in practice. I was speaking more and more at events and traveling all over Canada and the United States. My brokers were happy, my business functioned well, and I had plenty of money to do the things in life that I always thought I wanted to do.

I worked hard and made it a daily practice to strive for success.

I'm not entirely sure when it happened, but at some point, my striving shifted. Don't get me wrong, it didn't diminish. What happened was something a little more subtle. Slowly, somewhat imperceptibly, my ambition pivoted from chasing success to chasing significance. My values were shifting; I was starting to place less importance on the traditional definition of success. I started looking more at where I could make a difference in the world. Impact became my new currency.

Sometimes it is less about becoming the man you want to be and more about stepping into the man you already are.

I really don't know how or why this happened. I had always been a fairly right-wing capitalist, leading with head over heart almost exclusively. I'm not sure if it was the divorce, my new interest in yoga, or some unknown force that created the shift, but somewhere along the line it happened.

In 2014 I started a podcast. I thought that having a weekly outlet to share lessons and interview others would be a great way to foster my own growth. Around this time, I also started finding myself more interested in questions focused on "who people were" rather than "how they achieved what they achieved." Intellectually, I think I was starting to make the correlation between what made *them* and what made them successful, as opposed to simply what tactics or strategies people employed. I don't think it was even a conscious decision, but I started to look for ways to make my life matter in a meaningful way.

The previous year, in 2013, I had actually made one of my New Year's resolutions to actively look for opportunities to help people.

The more I helped others, the better I started to feel. At some point I decided to keep my own scorecard, a type of measure that was much healthier than what I had previously tallied with the frat boys of Eron. I could simply open up a spreadsheet and start making a list of individuals I had assisted, a list on which to reflect back at some point in the future, to inspire me to continue to help.

Then one of my podcast guests, Erik Giasson, who would go on to become a good friend, planted a tiny little seed in my mind: he talked about being present and engaged, about becoming aware of the world and taking the time to slow down and simply observe those around you. I started practicing paying attention to the names of the grocery clerks who assisted me; I started to write a paragraph in my head about my surroundings, noticing all the little details, the simple things. I started to realize that practice would allow me to hone these skills of observation and, therefore, more easily identify opportunities where I might be able to be of assistance.

Soon I moved the practice from awareness to action.

I used to get a coffee at the same place every morning as part of my ritualistic drive to work. I began paying for the order behind me every time I was in line at the drive thru. I didn't do it sporadically, or as some kind of justification or proof that I was a good human being when I needed validation. I did it every single day that I was in the drive thru, for about two years. The crew behind the counter started to recognize me, and I didn't even have to ask.

"Good morning, Mr. Mike," they would say and simply rattle off the total, including the vehicle behind me. It was fun, not only to be putting a smile on the face of the person behind me, but also to have the cashiers seemingly feel like they were a part of the goodness. They had figured out this practice as well.

One day as I was driving to the office after I had been home for lunch, I saw a young lady dressed in her work uniform walking up the street on her way to that same coffee shop. My house is about two kilometres from the store, not too far to walk but definitely a good haul. I recognized Cynthia as one of the ladies who frequently served me at the drive thru. Confident she would recognize my vehicle, I pulled over beside her, rolled down the window, and offered to give her a lift. She nodded and jumped in without hesitation. I had started to build relationships with the individuals who served me coffee every morning.

The point of the whole pay-it-forward in the drive thru was less about doing a good deed for one individual and more about building the habit of doing something nice for people in general, cultivating the behaviour that I wanted to pervade my entire life.

As a man who had always been goal oriented, I was finding that many of the work and life goals I continued to seek were not at all useful. In fact, they were actually harmful. So I made the decision to entirely stop setting goals, at least in the traditional manner.

Did it cost me? Have I achieved less? Sacrificed joy or productivity?

On the contrary, since that decision, my years have been the happiest and most productive of my life. Shifting my focus from doing to being was an absolute game changer. I'm sharing what works for me; I cannot speak to what may or may not work for you. All I can do is suggest that, if traditional goal setting is not getting you where you want to be, you might want to consider another way. I feel like I should have the small print, fast talking disclaimer here: "Results not typical and may vary from human being to human being. Changing your goal setting methodology is not a guarantee of happiness. If your methodology lasts for more than four hours, please consult your doctor." You know what I mean.

To me, success has always been about being just a little bit better today than I was yesterday.

Okay, that is not entirely true, as you know by now. In my twenties, I wanted to *have* all the stuff. I always managed to check the materialistic items — the big paycheck, the Boxster, the house — off my annual goal list. From that first six-figure income goal in my mid -twenties and beyond, I typically hit most of the financial milestones I put in front of myself, year after year. I had also had the family I always wanted: the beautiful wife, a daughter and son, and our life in the 'burbs. I had seemingly been living the dream.

There was still something missing. A lack of fulfilment. A missing piece of the puzzle. While I had convinced myself that meeting these goals was important to my personal development, I started to see that this was not really the case. Please don't get me wrong: I am extremely grateful for everything that has happened in my life. I have been blessed beyond all deserving. However, when I reflect on the happiest years of my life, I realize that contentment comes from having let go of some of those traditional goals.

You see, there are some inherent problems with the traditional model of goal setting that we don't always talk about. Let's explore these flaws.

TRADITIONAL GOALS LEAVE YOU OPEN FOR FAILURE

I know, I know, you are screaming it at the top of your lungs right now, "But, Mike! Failure is good! Failure is how we learn!" So let's get that out of the way. You are right, I agree with you 100%. I have nothing against failing; if you are not failing, you are not stepping far enough out of your comfort zone to do big things. But the problem with traditional goals is that they set a false measuring stick. Are you really a failure if you don't earn that six-figure income? Of course not. I am not opposed to having a wish list of material things, but we need to change what goes on the scorecard.

WHAT YOU *THINK* YOU WANT MAY NOT ACTUALLY *BE* WHAT YOU WANT

Let's take the six-figure income as an example again. It's probably not the amount, specifically, that you want. More likely, you want what you think that kind of income will allow you to have: the house, the car, the boat, the toys, the trips. Even those may not be your desired outcome. What you are really looking for is how those possessions will make you feel. Whether it is status, prestige, security, time with the family, or maybe just plain ol' fun, the income is really just a means to an end, not the end itself.

TRADITIONAL GOALS POTENTIALLY BLIND US TO OTHER POSSIBILITIES

If we are blindly focused on the means (the income, for example), we may actually miss other options to achieve our real desires. Even worse, the pursuit of those artificial goals may in fact take us further away from our true desires. If family time is your true priority, then trust me, chasing an income goal is probably the easiest way to get further and further away from that quality time. Somehow, we justify it in our tiny little brains: "I'm staying extra hours at the office so I can earn more income, so I can provide more for my family and have more time with them." Guess what? This isn't rocket science. If you want more time with your family, then spend *less* time at your job and *more* time with your family. That six-figure income goal may be in direct conflict with the real desired outcome.

YOU MAY NOT LIKE WHO YOU BECOME

Chasing materialistic goals may cause you to compromise your values as the justification for what the goal requires. Working extra hours may certainly get you that six-figure income, but does it come at the expense of missing your daughter's dance recital? Will you find yourself justifying a moral lapse that will get you that big deal?

We become too attached to the results

I know this one may seem counterintuitive. After all, aren't the results what matter? There are a number of perils in becoming results oriented:

When we focus on the results, we become future focused. We can easily miss out on the present. If instead we detach from the outcome and focus on the process or activities, we can become much more present focused. This shift allows us to more fully enjoy the moment instead of worrying about the potential future result.

When we focus on the result, we relinquish control. We have 100% control of the process we follow, but we do not necessarily have control of the results. There may be external factors that prevent us from ultimately achieving our desired outcome.

When you shift your mindset you take control.

When we become attached to the result, we tend to measure our worth by achievement rather than by effort. Effort is the only thing of which we have control.

We are less likely to experiment along the way. When we let go of the result, we are more apt to take a shot at other methodologies.

What is the alternative to traditional goal setting? My current version of the scorecard is comprised of three components: Values, Intentions, and Milestones.

First off, understand that most of what I have discovered has happened to me by accident. I wish I could say I had some sort of epiphany, that the skies parted and I had a vision, a divine message. But, nope, what follows are the changes in my process that evolved naturally, pulled out in hindsight. My hope is that you can take from my experiences the things that resonate with you and implement those things on purpose, rather than by trial and error.

The biggest strategy for me has been to really sit down and reflect on who I want to be. While values have always been important to me, I now make *who* I want to become a priority over *what* I want to have. This is the highest measure on my scorecard. Do I really give a shit if I don't hit my income target this year, so long as I can close out the year saying that I am closer to becoming the kind of man that I strive to be? Clearly, I don't.

The beauty of this kind of mindset is that it is all completely in your control. Think about that for a minute — all in *your* control. Things like income goals are out of our hands. Yes, we can have a significant impact on them, but if the market crashes, or people stop buying what you are selling, or your position gets cut, then those circumstances are beyond your control. We can, however, have full control of our thoughts and our actions which is essentially "who we are."

Acknowledging that values do change over time is important as well. I think we tend to think of values as static constants that should never change. I would be in a lot of trouble today if my current values were the same as they were for my 16-year-old self in Australia, or even my 20-something self back at Eron. Our experiences give us the opportunity to re-evaluate and revisit our values. When we challenge them, one of two things happen: either they are reinforced, or they start to change.

Over a lifetime, the values that continue to hold up to years of challenge and reflection are what ultimately shape who we are. The foundation of any action or plan is intention. While goals are future-focused, an intention is about the present moment. For me this is much more about who and how I want to be, as opposed to what I want to accomplish. I'll give you an example from my own life that demonstrates what I am talking about.

I love to climb — rock climbing, Ice climbing, or scrambling. When I go climbing, my goal might be to reach the summit. My intention, however, is to ensure I enjoy every moment of my surroundings and the beauty of the environment I am in and the company I am keeping. My intention is far more satisfying than my goal and can be achieved whether I make the summit or not.

Wrapping your head around setting an intention can be difficult. It can seem ethereal, intangible and like grasping at a cloud. Take a look at the following sentence starters and try a few on for size. Complete these sentences without a lot of deliberate thought and see what comes up for you. Try it a few times and see if it changes.

I want...

I intend...

I am...

I allow...

I open the possibility of...

Try completing the sentences above a few times and see what comes out. You may be surprised.

Milestones are much more akin to traditional goals but are waypoints along the journey. Here is where we can list the "things" we want to have or achieve, understanding that these are secondary to our values and intentions. In other words, we do not compromise values or intentions in order to achieve our milestones.

Here are some of the milestones I have set. I am happy to report I have hit all of them.

- Complete an Ironman triathlon
- Run a marathon
- Hold a headstand in yoga

- Do Crow pose
- Publish a book

I am still working on other milestones:

- Climb a 5.11
- Complete the Sinister 7 100 miler under 30 hours
- Get on a bestseller list

Now, will I hit all these milestones? Who cares?! The bottom line is by shifting my focus from *what* I want to have to *who* I want to become, I am assured success no matter the outcome.

This is exceedingly important because life can take away what you have, but it can never take away who you are. So focus on becoming more, not having more.

WHEN SOMETHING'S GOTTA CHANGE:

Simply changing our language from what we want to have to who we want to be can be a game changer.

Who do you want to be?

____

____

____

____

What are the guiding values that you want to shape that person?

____

____

____

____

CHAPTER 19

EMBRACE THE SUCK

Part of becoming who I really am meant getting in touch with my physical self. You see, I was never what you'd call the athletic type, but I did enjoy running and staying in shape, and it's a trait I passed along to my kids. In June of 2012, my then 12-year-old son had us register him for the Edmonton ITU triathlon in the Kids of Steel division. Chris had been competing recreationally in triathlons since the age of seven. Those early short-run competitions when the kids were still very small were some of the cutest things you have ever seen.

My daughter Mikaela followed Christopher's and my lead at a young age — she was five when she rode her first race. I remember running beside her on her bike with its little basket on the front, cheering her on. With her trademark smile shining brightly on her delicate face, she pedalled with an enthusiasm for life that too many seem to lose along the way to adulthood. She looked up at me running beside her at one point and exclaimed, "This is fun! Can we do it again tomorrow?" Laughing, I encouraged her to finish the event in which she was currently participating.

By the beginning of 2012, Christopher had moved up to the U13 level, and the distances were starting to get a little bit more real. On this June day he swam 500 meters open water, cycled a full 15 kilometres, and ended with a 3-kilometre run. I will never forget walking alongside the pack of young athletes down to the water, trying to get a photo of my boy as the race started. It was a proud papa moment to be certain. Chris was a good head shorter than most of the boys, his late birthday ensuring he was one of the youngest in the category. The athletes were led by a bagpiper from the staging area down to the start line, with all the pomp and ceremony of an Olympic event. Chris had his game face on and wasn't going to mug for the camera. It honestly choked me up a little watching the scene unfold.

I thought my heart might burst when I watched him coming up the finisher's chute, turning on the jets for that final push to cross the finish line. It was a hot day and he had left it all out there on the course. He was bright red from exertion, but he proudly touched the medal around his neck. I gave him a big high five and sweaty hug. In his typical fashion, he started to breathlessly recount the entire race for me, recalling the scrum of the swim and the hills on the bike, his mouth going a mile a minute with exhilaration and evident pride in his accomplishment. He confided that he felt he did not have a great run, but overall he was happy.

Then he stopped and looked at me. "Dad, you should do Kelowna with me."

Kelowna was a race in British Columbia held in August that we had talked about doing before. We spent most summers at my parents' place in Hope, BC, so it would be local. I looked into his eyes, which shone with pride and accomplishment. What else could my response be?

"Of course I will do Kelowna with you!"

I knew the Kelowna race had a "try-a-tri," which was a shorter distance event for newbies. I justified my knee-jerk enthusiasm with logic: I had run a marathon before, after all. So I had never really done a swim, but, hey, it was only 300 meters. How hard could that be?

My immediate response was a perfect example of a truth I had learned from twenty years in sales. We make decisions on emotion, justified by logic.

An hour later, the reality sank in: I couldn't swim.

Well, that's not quite true. Like many kids, I had splashed around in pools and lakes for years. I had also done some swimming lessons as a child, but now as an adult, to swim 300 metres? While I theoretically knew how to do the front crawl, it was an entirely different thing actually doing it. I could barely go 25 metres without choking on pool water and immediately hacking out my lung.

I am not too proud to admit it: I was scared. Three hundred metres was starting to look like 100 miles.

So, like any tech savvy individual, I knew exactly what to do. I Googled it. I found a program that helped you to stretch your breathing just a little bit each time, not worrying about form or technique but getting your lungs conditioned to consume the oxygen you needed. Basically, the idea was just to get the distance in any way you could and to keep the rests short enough that you weren't quite entirely recovered before starting the next lap.

You have to suck before you can succeed.

Within a few weeks, I became comfortable with the breathing aspect and could then focus on technique. In the two months or so I had to prepare for the race, I could now comfortably (if not quickly) swim the 300 metres required to compete.

Of course, from there I went on to get proper coaching on form and technique and am now a fairly strong swimmer. What I learned from this experience is this:

No one is born good at something. You have to suck at it first and practice to become proficient. In the end I managed to get through the Kelowna Apple Try-a-tri and fell in love with the sport.

Believe me when I say that, as I advanced through my triathlon training and events, the concept of something "sucking" became very familiar. Not that I was entirely horrible at the event, but I did have to take my tolerance for pain and discomfort to a whole new level. I found to be true what Chris "Macca" McCormack, two-time winner of the Ironman World Championship, says: "The difference between a good race and a bad race is how you manage the (inevitable) pain."

In 2013, I completed my first Iron Distance triathlon. In the lead up and training to complete that race, I started paying a lot of attention to those who had been there before me — my coach, other triathletes that I knew, and especially the pro field of triathletes that graced the covers of the triathlon magazines I had started reading. Macca soon became one of my favourites. In early 2013, he published an article entitled "Embrace the Suck." The quote above is his opening line, and that statement moved me from the category of "nervous" into a new state of sheer terror about what I was going to attempt to accomplish.

In the article, Macca talks about his move from short distance triathlon to long course, Ironman racing. He explains that, in an Ironman, the pain is inevitable. Unlike short course races, where he would simply put his head down and push through the discomfort of that last ten minutes of the race, in a full Ironman his pain was more than just physical. A mental fatigue for which he had not prepared crept in as well. He also talked about the fact that no amount of physical training is going to allow you to bypass the suck, to avoid the pain. It is something you have to accept and embrace.

Do you think the sentiment might apply to the world of pain and ensuing negative emotions that life throws at us from time to time? If success in long distance triathlon depends on your ability to manage pain, then perhaps the same holds true for the inevitable "suck" we all experience, the external events that may or may not be under our control and that manifest themselves as a stew of emotions. Our natural instinct is to avoid these events in order to avoid the negative emotions that come with them.

As Macca explains in his article, he soon realized with long distance triathlon that there simply was no amount of preparation, no amount or type of training, that was going to allow him to avoid the pain that comes with the gruelling effort. He concludes that, rather than focusing on how to avoid it, we need to find a way to embrace and manage the pain. "You have to start planning for pain and understand how you deal with it when it comes," he says.

This advice holds equally true for life.

There is simply no amount of life preparation, no amount of caution that you can take that will allow you to avoid pain in your life. Whatever that situation is — the dissolution of a relationship, a job loss, a business failure, an unfavourable medical diagnosis, or the death of someone we love — some pain in life is simply inevitable. Therefore, the quality of our lives becomes directly connected to how well we manage that pain. The earlier we accept and recognize that pain is unavoidable, the more effort and emphasis we can put on learning how to manage these emotions — as opposed to avoiding them.

It has been my experience that the more I fight the negative emotions when they strike (and trust me, I'm a fighter, so this is hard), the more I try to make them disappear, the longer they stick around. Instead, I have learned to allow myself to recognize the emotions and to say, "Here comes the suck, baby!" Then I can step outside of the feelings and really analyze the thoughts and baggage that accompany them. In doing this, I circumvent the compounding effect of having the negatives snowball, building on one another, instead of dissipating. I'm actually able to let the emotions run their course. I can observe and I can learn.

The more I can objectively do this, the more skilled I become at understanding and managing my emotions. The result is that the duration of these negative emotions becomes shorter and shorter.

Once again, it comes down to the fact that we all have choices. We can choose to accept that we "suck" and never get up off that couch. Or we can choose to accept that we suck, acknowledge it without judgement or self-deprecation, and make the decision to change. I realize that making the choice to change can be daunting. It requires us to become vulnerable again and possibly allow people to see just how *much* we suck at something. Keep in mind that sucking at something may be different for everyone, yet the options we have are all the same. Whether you are looking at doing an Ironman, or whether you simply need to get off the couch and go for a walk — it all starts with a decision.

My next challenge was to get off the loveseat and let myself love again.

WHEN SOMETHING'S GOTTA CHANGE:

Creating opportunities to practice "embracing the suck" allows us to prepare in a controlled environment. For me, putting myself in uncomfortable physical challenges was one of the ways I created those opportunities.

Where do you find opportunities to practice?

___

___

___

___

Where can you actively create more opportunities to "embrace the suck" in a somewhat controlled environment?

___

___

___

___

CHAPTER 20

SWIPING RIGHT

After I moved out of our matrimonial home, I ultimately purchased a house five minutes away, so that I could create a home base for myself but be close enough that the disruption to the kids would be minimal. Christine and I shared custody; I had the kids for a week at a time every other week.

I spent the bulk of the first few years really working on myself. I found yoga and meditation, both of which really helped me move out of my head and much more into my heart. Instead of spending much time dating, I had instead tried to focus inward and sort out what this new life would look like.

There are pivotal moments in your life. Some take you by surprise and alter your path in big ways, like glaring billboards too prominent to miss. Others aren't so obvious at the time. I have become acutely aware of these less obvious moments. I embrace them and find as much meaning in them as I possibly can.

My first venture into the new world of dating happened when I was out for a beer with a female friend. We sat in a side booth in a seedy, low-lit pool hall with a couple of pints of draft served by a waitress who was wearing far less than what the weather called for. The music just a bit too loud, the sound of pool balls cracking in the background — if you paid attention you could smell the sense of loneliness in the air. One might think the setting ripe for the opportunity to find another lonely soul looking for love.

That is not exactly how it happened. Instead, my friend asked me if I was on Tinder. Now, I am a technology enthusiast and certainly not unworldly, so we were both surprised to learn that I did not even know what Tinder was. I was intrigued, and lonely, and (after another round of beers) agreed to let her set up a profile for me on my phone. She selected the images to use for my profile and created my description. Then, much to my horror, she started swiping. Tinder is really all about the pictures. Who reads the profile description? She went through the profiles of the women in our vicinity and started "right swiping" ones that she thought "might be good for me." We laughed over this for a little while, until she had exhausted the potential matches in my pre-defined radius. We finished our drinks and I caught a cab home, completely dismissing the whole Tinder app incident as if it never happened.

The next morning when I woke up and looked at my phone, I was intrigued to see that I had a few matches. I opened the app and had a look. The first match was an attractive woman with some great photos but not much else to tell me about her. I thought, "What the heck, let's take a chance." So I sent her a message. I don't recall exactly what I said, but it was polite, respectful, and probably very naive.

After I sent the message, I went back in and had a look at the next match. I was mortified to see that it was a past client of mine who was also a Facebook friend. As attractive as she was, she was certainly not someone on whom I would have swiped right, for fear of exactly the awkwardness that I now faced.

Note to self: Don't let friends handle your Tinder account. Ever.

So I did what I often do in awkward situations: I ignored it and hoped it would go away.

Later that day, I received a response from my first match. We exchanged some pleasantries, and I confessed to not having a clue what I was doing here. Tinder was widely thought of as a "hook-up" app, but at this point in the game, I still had no idea what I was getting into or what common abbreviations on the site like DTF — "down to fuck" — meant. She commented that I was quite different than most of the men on the app. I gathered she meant I was polite. I assumed this was a good thing and would bode well for me as I explored this possible relationship.

Yeah, I was wrong. Man was I ever wrong.

She went on to explain that she was in an open marriage and that she and her husband liked exploring other sexual relationships.

Wait, what?

Don't get me wrong, I'm no prude and certainly do not judge lifestyle choices, but this was more than I was ready for after being out of the dating game for 15 years. I said a polite goodbye and quickly deleted the app from my phone.

So I was done with dating sites for the time being. Yet a guy still needs companionship, so when an old friend messaged me and asked if I would be interested in meeting a friend of hers for a date, I readily agreed. I certainly wasn't looking for a relationship at that point in time, but I am always game to meet new people. The reality was that I needed some kind of distraction. Some companionship would take my mind off some of the more pressing things in life. Like most things these days, the introduction happened virtually and eventually we ended up exchanging phone numbers.

The night of our first date, we were sitting in her living room drinking wine, when all of a sudden, it hit me: she was waiting for me to make a move! Holy shit. I wasn't sure I had any moves left. After all, it had been well over 15 years since I had even kissed anyone other than my wife. What the hell was I supposed to do? So I did what many of us men do when we don't know what to do.

I did nothing and had another drink.

In December of 2014, I had something of an epiphany.

I had been separated for two years and eight months. I had spent much of that time in self-reflection and had continued on my journey of self-discovery. I felt like I was finally free to become the man I was supposed to be, and I felt fantastic.

I was at our company Christmas party down in Calgary. Every December, Axiom Mortgage hosts a wonderful dinner event at a private venue — first class all the way — and this particular year, we had a private room with an open bar and dining area where we could enjoy a fabulous meal. We truly had some of the most wonderful people working with us, and the night was an opportunity to celebrate our collective accomplishments and simply enjoy each other's company. If you've ever partied with a mortgage broker, then you know that providing an open bar was a questionable decision. We stayed well after dark and well after all the food was gone, mixing and mingling and recounting stories of the year gone by and sharing excited anticipation for the year to come.

I struck up a conversation with one of our mortgage associates, Christina, who likes to test me a little and who enjoys being just flirtatious enough to make me squirm a bit. People tend to look at me and make assumptions based on my generally outgoing nature, apparent confidence, and success by traditional definitions. But while I'm great if you put me in front of a room of 500 with a message to deliver, I can sometimes be a little bit shy in an individual setting, especially when it comes to going toe-to-toe with someone who is attractive, charismatic, and extremely outgoing.

The trouble with being an introverted extrovert is that sometimes my behaviour can be misconstrued as either indifference or social awkwardness.

Christina and I ended up having a very good conversation about my social insecurity despite my outwardly confident demeanour. It was a very deep and meaningful conversation and certainly not one I would have expected to have with Christina. While I had considered her a friend for many years, we'd never really had much in the way of meaningful conversation beyond the work environment. I found the depth, intellect, and challenging nature of the conversation refreshing and intriguing.

Like most stereotypical Christmas parties, there were a few who had a little more "fun" than others. I knew that there would be some "Christmas shame" being felt hard and heavy the next morning. My business partner Gord has a saying of which I am particularly fond. He says, "In this village, we have no idiot. Here we all take turns." Thankfully, that Christmas was not my turn. After talking late and eventually branching back to the core group, I headed back to my hotel, well into the wee hours of the morning, for some shut eye before I had to make the three-hour commute home the next morning.

I typically used the long drive home to make a few phone calls, sometimes just to reassure those who might have expressed themselves (due to the liquid courage served at the party) a tad more than what might be deemed socially appropriate that it was all okay. I liked to assure them there was no judgement, and certainly no one has ever done or said anything inappropriate enough for any kind of reprimand. That year there were some relieved voices on the other end of the line.

When it came time to call Christina to thank her for coming and tell her how much I enjoyed the conversation, I was surprised to find that the conversation simply picked back up where we left off. I think we chatted for a good hour out of that three-hour commute. Once again, I was intrigued to see how much I enjoyed conversation with this woman.

I had very little interest in pursuing another relationship, as I was really enjoying the progress I had been making on my own personal development. While I had dated over those two and a half years, anytime it started looking like the relationship was going down the path toward something more serious, I always found a reason why the person I was dating wasn't "my" person. I really just could not even come close to wrapping my head around the possibility of calling someone my girlfriend.

So it was definitely a surprise when I found myself on the phone with Christina on many occasions over the following days, discussing everything from yoga and meditation to our musical tastes. There was no doubt some kind of connection. We often stayed on the phone together for hours, usually talking well past midnight. I started to realize how wonderful it would be to share my newfound peace and comfort with someone all the time.

Shortly after New Year's, when Christina and I had again spent the bulk of the evening on the phone together, she booked a trip to Mexico with a girlfriend. The first night she was away, I got the drunken video call. I was thrilled! I already missed her. We had a fun, tequila-induced conversation that didn't last all that long, but we did not talk again during her trip.

When she got home, we had a few more conversations but we both seemed to recognize that it was going nowhere. So we let it fade.

They say people come into your life for a reason. While I enjoyed our camaraderie very much, I had no delusions about the possibility of a meaningful romantic relationship with Christina. She had never been married, never had kids, and clearly wanted both. We were at very different stages of our lives; I could not provide her with what she wanted — and I would never have deprived her of her heart's desires.

The pivotal part of this experience for me was that Christina fanned the flames of a fire I did not even realize was burning. That encounter unlocked a part of my heart that had been shut down for many years. My life was fantastic — and I wanted more than ever to share it with someone in a meaningful way. My love life was a flower about to blossom and simply needed a little bit of food and water. I will be forever grateful for the nourishment Christina provided me.

It had now been almost three years since my separation, but I was ready: it was time to expand my horizons, open my field of view, and dip my toes back in the water.

Then it occurred to me that I had to dangle my line in the murky waters of dating at 45 years old. And I'd probably have to go back online. Scary.

WHEN SOMETHING'S GOTTA CHANGE:

The quality of our lives is the quality of our relationships. We have numerous opportunities to evaluate and address the relationships in our lives.

How honest are you being with yourself about your relationship status?

____

____

____

____

If you're ready for more out of your relationships, what's holding you back?

____

____

____

____

CHAPTER 21

DATING DO OVER

I have to admit that the idea of serious dating again, after 15 years of marriage and three years of waiting, both excited and scared the shit out of me. The thought of having to wade through the variety of singles at this age, all of whom would have some kind of story (i.e., baggage like mine) was not really an appealing idea. On the other hand, the prospect of a new adventure at every outing appealed to my intrepid nature. I wasn't sure I was ready for dating again. Fortunately, I had some persuasive friends.

Eventually, with the encouragement of my assistant Shawna, I set up a free profile on Match.com. I admit I was nervous at the start, but I also figured I was probably a pretty good catch who would likely stack up well against my competition — and yes, at this point, every other single male on the planet instantly felt like my competition. But I was a successful, mature man who had his shit together, for the most part. I was financially secure and, while I would never be mistaken for Brad Pitt or Ryan Gosling, after three years of hard physical training and paying attention to my overall fitness levels, I had never felt more confident in my life.

I was ready for an adventure.

And man did I ever get one.

My first real post-marriage dating experience was a bit of a train wreck. As a novice at online dating, I didn't yet know the red flags to watch out for. See if you can spot them, where I couldn't in the moment.

I was drawn to Kerri's profile for a few reasons: first off, she was very attractive, obviously the first thing you notice when you are seeking a potential match online. Her profile was well-written. She talked about how much yoga had become an important part of her life. Having found yoga only six months earlier myself, this spoke to me. I also really liked all of the things she talked about as being important in a relationship: mutual respect, trust, personal development, and growth. All that coupled with an extremely attractive set of photos ensured that I took the time to reach out.

After the Tinder experiment, I was feeling less than optimistic, telling myself that I was out of my league and not likely to get a response. After a day or two had passed and I had not heard back from her or found what I would have deemed a comparable or equally intriguing profile, I decided to go all in, so to speak.

I sat down and wrote a fairly long message to her that expanded on my views of each of the qualities or characteristics that she had written about as important in her profile. I ended up with close to 2000 words and realized that one of two things would happen: either she would ignore it as complete drivel and not invest the time to read the entire thing, or else she would be so impressed with my thoughtfulness that she would be compelled to respond. Fortunately for me, the latter of the two options happened and she responded with a "Wow."

I didn't know at that time but found out later that my competition from other men online usually consisted of an email that said, "Hey hottie whatcha doin?"

I had certainly thought about how to attract a woman but had opted to take the approach of just putting my true self out there. Now I had been rewarded with a response. I decided at that moment that I was not going to waste time trying to impress a woman by presenting the version of myself that I thought she *wanted* to see.

This fairly simple concept was not something I immediately recognized. After all, why bother putting up a front that would eventually come down, leaving you with the prospect of losing that relationship when the real you surfaced anyhow?

At this stage in my life I was not really interested in trying to fake it to be with someone, no longer that guy who'd wanted so desperately to fit into Frank's circle. While this is an easy concept to grasp intellectually, it is actually much harder to practice. The reality was that I was more likely to find the right person that much faster if I let my guard down early and simply presented the whole version of myself — the good, the bad, and the ugly. Now, don't get me wrong, I wouldn't suggest you go around farting in public on your first date, but certainly it is worth letting yourself "be seen," so to speak.

After my Tinder experience I was less than optimistic.

Kerri and I had some fabulous conversations online while trying to carve out a time to meet face to face. We had a couple of failed attempts where our kids' schedules or some other such thing got in the way, so we rescheduled more than once. Eventually, we booked a dinner date on a Sunday evening at a local restaurant.

I was extremely pleased to see that her photos did not lie when Kerri walked through that door. We had a nice, easy rapport, and I laughed when she opened with "I am supposed to go to a movie with my girlfriend a little later," realizing the setup for an easy out had I not been much in the way of good company. I actually called her on it later in the evening when she "got a text" from her girlfriend cancelling. I joked that I had obviously passed the first test and, clearly, she wanted to spend more time with me.

We shared similar work experiences, and both of us were avidly into the field of personal growth and development. The conversation was easy, so easy that I did not want it to end. When we did end up finishing dinner, I suggested we head somewhere else for a beer. I also let her know that I had a flight to catch to Vancouver the next morning at 7 a.m. for a conference, so I couldn't really stay out all that late. She agreed and we went to a local pub nearby for a beer and a game of pool.

When we got there, a lone man sat at the bar, noticeable because of the intense conversation he was having with the bartender. He seemed to me to be an obvious regular who preferred the company of strangers over his own company sitting at home alone. He was thin and in his late 50s or early 60s, although his face, likely aged by alcohol, made it difficult to say for sure.

Kerri and I ordered beers at the bar and gathered some change to play pool. Shortly after starting our game, this gentleman came over from the bar and asked to play the winner. I looked at my date to read her expression, and I could see the same kind of compassion on her face that I felt. Here was a man, alone and lonely, looking for comfort in the company of strangers. I nodded to him and said we would love to have him play the winner.

Imagine what the world might look like if we could all be a little more compassionate to those around us.

Since my divorce, I had been trying hard to lead more with my heart then my head. And if I'm being completely honest, I was likely playing up my newfound compassion for humankind to impress Kerri just the tiniest bit.

We played a few games with this man and had some interesting conversation. He lived in the condominiums behind the complex we were in, and he was divorced, alone, and clearly an alcoholic. I was pleased we could offer him a little bit of warmth for the evening. I did eventually explain to him that we were on our first date and were going to retire to a booth alone to visit. Thankfully, he was very gracious and took the hint without further need for clarification. It was back in that booth where we enjoyed our first, wonderful kiss. As I've already established, I'm a slow mover, so I'm sure Kerri instigated the kiss.

By this time, we were at last call and it was now close to 2 a.m. My early morning flight was looming, but I was resigned to not getting much sleep, as I was having a wonderful evening. We ended up back in her vehicle in the parking lot after the bar closed where we sat, talked, and made out for another hour before I decided that I should probably get home, pack, and have a brief power nap before getting on the road to the airport.

I packed in a blur, grabbed that nap, and made my way to the airport. I was off to the Mortgage Brokers Association of British Columbia conference. This conference was a late addition to my schedule, and when I got to the hotel, I found that the only room left for my assistant to book had been a two-bedroom suite.

I had been texting (and flirting) with Kerri a good chunk of the morning. I admit it was fun finding a little bit of that romantic spark again. When I got to my hotel room, I messaged her a picture of the two bedroom doors and said, "My assistant had to book a two-bedroom suite. A little too much room for one. Want to join me?"

She replied with, "Are you serious?"

I hadn't been, but I thought, why not? When I replied in the affirmative, she responded that she had the next day off and would see if she could get the following day off as well. I had my assistant look at flight options, and we found one that would work well. Before I really had time to think about it, Kerri's flight was booked.

Keep in mind this was still my first real dating experience after marriage, and I wanted to ensure there were no awkward expectations or ambiguous intentions for the next few days. So I told Kerri there was a condition we would have to meet if she were to come out.

No sex.

Truth be told, I was still pretty nervous in that department, and this way I could take any unwanted pressure off. She said that she had to do a little bit of shopping and asked if there was anything that I needed before she arrived. I told her that I had forgotten to pack much of anything other than the suits I would be wearing for the conference and asked if she could pick me up a pair of pajamas. She agreed to do that, and I set off to the first sessions of the conference buzzing with the anticipation of picking her up later that night.

After dinner, I went to meet Kerri's arriving flight. The butterflies in my stomach wrestled with the logic in my head that was questioning what was happening. Those butterflies are a lot tougher than you might think. I had still not recovered from my lack of sleep and felt quite giddy, but I was not 100 percent certain I would even recognize her coming off the plane. Fortunately, that did not turn out to be a problem.

Back at the hotel, instead of taking the vacant room, she moved herself right into my room. Clearly, she had taken my condition of not sleeping together more along the lines of a challenge to overcome rather than a condition to be met.

As she unpacked with her back to me, she said, "Oh, I picked you up some pajamas." She turned around holding a pair of bright pink boxer briefs, a grin the size of New York spread across her face. Yes, I was starting to see that this was going to be a challenge indeed.

We were scheduled to join some of my industry friends at the lounge a little later, and Kerri asked if I minded if she had a shower before we left. She then proceeded to strip down to her underwear before heading into the bathroom. The playful smirk on her face indicated that she was enjoying herself.

I will spare you all of the details for the next few days, but I assure you that my integrity remained intact and my commitment held.

During our stay, we had decided to hit a yoga studio close to the hotel, and after realizing that I had not brought any shorts at all, I called the studio to see if they had a retail outlet where I could buy some. When I was assured that they did in fact have one, we hopped on the sky train, Vancouver's public transit, and set off for the studio. But when we got to the studio, we found that their retail outlet had been closed for renovations and did not have any inventory.

This provided a bit of a dilemma but also an opportunity to show my true authentic self. There were a couple of things going for me that day, though. First off, I was wearing the pink boxers Kerri had brought for my pajamas. Second, it was Pink Shirt Day, which promoted anti-bullying. And third, I was not likely to run into anyone at the Richmond Studio whom I would know or ever see again.

Another step out of my comfort zone. I made the decision to do this hot yoga practice in my bright pink boxers.

Feeling quite self-conscious, I made my way from the changing room, somewhat dismayed to see that the room was quite bright. There would be no hiding in a dim corner. In fact, as I was soon to realize was typical of her character, my partner in crime had selected two spots right smack in the middle of the studio floor.

Our first date ended three days after it had begun. I was a little bit on cloud nine. The few days were just incredibly comfortable and easy. There was no feeling of tension at all. This was the beginning of what I thought was to be a very long and healthy relationship.

Over the course of the next few months, Kerri and I had some amazing times together and the relationship grew. Still, there were moments that should have given me some clues, like the time we went to West Edmonton Mall to take in a comedy show.

We had a few drinks and an appetizer before we went into the comedy show. It was shaping up to be a nice night out. Then, somewhere between drinks and the comedy show, she uttered the words "I love you." I am not entirely sure of the context, but think I said something to the effect of "Thank you."

Spoiler alert: my response did not enhance the mood of the evening.

When we went into the comedy show, I was receiving the full-on cold shoulder. The drinks started to come faster and faster as the mood got more and more tense. Then the comedian made a joke related to special needs kids. It was a little edgy but not overtly disrespectful or distasteful.

Have I mentioned that Kerri has a disabled child? Especially with the amount of alcohol involved and the already-tense mood, I knew the joke wasn't going to go over well. Sure enough, she called him out on it, and the poor guy was in a no-win situation. This was not a standard heckler — this was a protective, drunk mother of a special needs kid who had been offended.

Both the comedian and I managed to make it through the event. My cab ride home with Kerri was awkward to say the least, exacerbated by the alcohol and the comedian, and was the scene of the first of a few incoherent and incomprehensible conversations we would have. She kept talking in circles, and I could not get anywhere. There was no discussion to be had; she seemed intent on making this one epic fight. I was completely confused. I think she was offended by the fact that I did not reciprocate the *I love you,* though I am not entirely sure. The night ended with a long discussion that went nowhere, until eventually we went to sleep. I was left wondering what the hell had happened. The next morning, though, it seemed that everything was back to normal, and I was left scratching my head.

The next few weeks were a continuation of the emotional roller coaster of the comedy night, shifting from extreme highs to extreme lows. In one case, I had been out of town for a few days and received a text from Kerri as I was about to drive home. I dialled immediately so we could have a phone conversation while I drove. I was hoping to be able to see her that evening.

She did not answer the phone. I thought it odd, given that she had texted not 30 seconds earlier. I did not hear back from her the rest of the night. Bizarre, I thought.

I was starting to fall in love — or so I thought — but was really struggling with the high and low intensity. In some ways Kerri and I seemed perfect together, and then when we were apart, the distance seemed vast.

Just Like That It Was Over

Our relationship came to a surprising conclusion the night Marilyn Manson was in town. The opening act was the daughter of one of our lending suppliers, and I loved the headliner, so I made plans to go with a colleague.

I like to try and make an experience out of most activities, to make them noteworthy as best I can. So when Marilyn Manson came to town, my 46-year-old self did indeed make my best attempt at being a 20-something-year-old goth. I picked up black jeans and a leather jacket to go with my Ozzy Osbourne t-shirt, along with black eyeliner, lipstick, and nail polish, and headed home to get ready for the evening. At some point, I sent a pic to my 12-year-old daughter, whose immediate reaction was, "Are you using my black nail polish?"

to which I quickly replied, "No, I bought my own." Her next reaction was predictable: "You look weird."

"Thanks, sweetie," I texted back, "I love you, too."

My buddy and I had agreed to meet at a pub downtown for a few pre-show drinks then walk over to the concert venue. I think we were both a little hesitant to be seen in public in our getups.

As I drove downtown, I got a call from Kerri, who had just finished work and called to check up on me. I had not planned to see her that evening, as it was her night with her kid and I had the concert. She sounded disappointed when I reminded her about the concert. When I pressed, she said she had arranged for a babysitter for the night and was hoping that we could go to a movie together. I was genuinely disappointed. I invited her to come down for a drink with us before the show, but she declined because she still had to pick up her child from school.

My friend and I met for our beer. Our server was quick to recognize the getup as a segue to the concert and confided she wished she was able to go. She even paid a few compliments on my makeup job (clearly playing to my insecure little ego for tips, but hey, I would take what I could get).

Someone dressed in goth attire is not unheard of for downtown Edmonton, certainly not out of character on a night when several thousand fans descended upon downtown to rock out with Die Mannequin and Marilyn Manson. Still, I felt sheepish and extremely out of place — yet somehow liberated.

There is something to be said for being in costume. I think it helps you to drop the virtual mask that you often wear to feel more accepted. You're already pretending to be someone else on the outside, so why bother pretending to be someone else on the inside too? You can allow the real inner you to shine through.

I had a glow about me that evening. I felt alive; I felt on fire.

This was going to be a night of epic proportions; I could feel it in my bones. I would drop my mask and let inhibition go and release everything to the world.

After powering down a few cocktails, we headed out onto the street to find the horde of goth and goth wannabes en route to the concert venue a few short blocks away. We arrived early to catch up with my friend's daughter Care Failure (or Caroline Kawa, as I knew her) for a quick hello and selfie so we could send a pic to her Dad letting him know we had connected with his little girl.

Then we filtered into the show area, making our way to a large bar at the back of the floor to fuel up with a beer before things kicked off. Soon after our refuel, the lights dimmed, smoke flowed, strobes flashed, and Die Mannequin hit the stage with a bang. I was not expecting a lot from Die Mannequin but they absolutely kicked ass. Their recent single "Sucker Punch" was a knockout.

Little did I know it would be somewhat prophetic for the night.

Marilyn Manson did not disappoint. Emerging from a shroud of special effect fog, face painted like a tribal zombie floating on stage to Mozart's requiem, Marilyn opened the show with "Deep Six." The raw energy in the air was palpable, drawing me into the mosh pit like a vortex. I quickly lost my friend as I pushed deep into the throng surging against the stage, writhing to the beat of the Pale Emperor. I was determined to drink in as much of the experience as I possibly could. Part of me wanted to push deeper in, part of me fought claustrophobia as the crush of the crowd grew stronger. The concrete floor was slick with spilled alcohol; an errant bump, a misplaced foot, and down I went. My perspective seemed to switch to slow motion as my view changed from looking out to looking up. But any misgivings about my fellow goths trampling me were wildly unfounded. As soon as I hit the floor an opening appeared and several pairs of hands were on me, quickly scooping me back to vertical.

An hour and a half later when the smoke cleared and the lights came up, I was on cloud nine. In the throng, I quickly gave up any hope of finding my friend. Once outside, I hopped in the first cab I could find, messaging Kerri to see if she had changed her mind about a visit.

She was aloof and I was a little weirded out by the whole exchange. I didn't understand. She was in love with me, and I was starting to fall in love with her too. Why wouldn't she want to spend time together? Post beers and concert, my Spidey sense was screaming at me. Once again, she had gone from an extreme high of wanting to be together to this state of what felt like total indifference.

I didn't understand. Weren't we in love?

I messaged her several times that I was going to come over, even if just for a quick visit. The vehemence of her refusal to see me and the way she quickly turned the issue into a fight left me at a complete loss.

I decided that I had to go to her house. I wanted to demonstrate my loyalty and devotion. A little blinded by "Love," my strong desire to have a relationship this romantic was not to be denied. Quite drunk and clearly not thinking straight, I would accept that she did not want to see me, but decided I would go to her house and leave her a little note in the mailbox for the morning.

The cab dropped me at home, where I grabbed a pen and a paper. Overlooking the cold temperatures and the snow that had fallen earlier in the day, armed with writing supplies, I set off at a drunken jog to cover the near five kilometres to her house. How moved would she be the next morning when she woke to find a love note in her mailbox? Clearly my intent could not be questioned.

It seems my naivety knew no bounds. When I got to her house, I saw that there was a truck parked on the street; a clear set of footprints in the snow led up to the front door. In the span of a second, I went from lovesick puppy dog to heartbroken. All of the courage that I had taken three years to muster putting myself out there again was shattered.

Unfortunately, in the light of the next day, I had no choice but to recognize the evidence for what it was: Kerri was cheating on me and probably had been for some time.

And just like that, my first relationship after my marriage was over.

Putting myself out there and getting burnt so badly, after taking so much time to prepare myself to start dating again, was certainly a devastating blow. It only added to my confusion about love and the ephemeral nature of our emotions. Was there really such a thing as true love? Or were we destined to float through life finding the next one rather than THE one?

I was heartbroken, confused, and back at square one. With my first substantial attempt at love online thwarted, I gained some experience and an extremely valuable lesson on what I wanted and what I would not tolerate. It was another lesson in trusting my gut.

Fortunately for me, I summoned up enough courage to continue my pursuit of companionship. It turned out to be one of the best decisions of my life.

WHEN SOMETHING'S GOTTA CHANGE:

I could have easily let this setback hold me back and inhibit forward progress. Life isn't about being fearless; it is about being courageous.

What are the areas in your life where you have had setbacks that you need to summon some courage to move through?

____

____

____

____

What could your life look like if you were able to move forward regardless of your fears?

____

____

____

____

CHAPTER 22

STOP TRYING

I had accepted the notion that even the best of the best sucked at their craft at some point in time. The realization made it so much easier for me to move forward with the myriad of endeavours that I had dreamed up for myself.

Specifically, I had started listening to podcasts and was enamoured with the interview format. What an excellent opportunity to learn and grow through the lessons of others, I decided. The more I listened, the more I loved the simplicity of the medium. I realized that with the technology available to me, it would be extremely easy to emulate what I was listening to. I could use the podcast format on a weekly basis to record lessons I was learning to identify for myself.

The advantage was twofold: one, it would force me to look for and articulate lessons every week, and two, it would give me an opportunity to practice what I love: speaking. So, yes, I made the decision to start a podcast of my own.

At first, I wasn't sure I would even share the recordings with anyone, or whether I would simply use it as a practice ground for personal development. In the end, I did start sharing what I had done. It was not an easy thing to do by any stretch.

I worry a little bit in the writing of my journey that it sounds as if all of the things I have attempted have come naturally and are therefore inaccessible to others. Nothing could be further from the truth. I have had to work hard for almost everything that I have done in my life: the business, the family, the fitness, and most importantly, the relationships.

It was incredibly difficult to finally accept the work that I had done in the first couple of episodes, as, frankly, they sucked. They were certainly not my best work, but I had to accept that and make the decision to move forward, knowing that I would improve in subsequent attempts. For me, this is the exciting part of starting a new endeavour: knowing your improvement will be quick because you are starting from zero.

One of my favourite podcasts at the time was *Six Pixels of Separation* by Mitch Joel. It was a marketing podcast, and his monologues and interviews set a standard that I aspired to achieve. Mitch was on something like Episode 426 when I started listening to him. But one of the best things that I ever did was to go back and listen to his first episode. You may or may not be surprised to learn that it really wasn't all that good. Who knew? Even the endeavours that you admire today likely sucked in their draft stage. This gave me a lot of hope that the quality of my podcast would continue to improve.

The main barrier to progress is not a lack of knowledge; it is a lack of application of that knowledge.

Finding someone you admire and looking at some of their early work is an excellent exercise, no matter what endeavour you are considering. We often hear the advice to find someone who is good at what we want to do and emulate them. I mean, why recreate the wheel, right? While this is an excellent suggestion, the *better* exercise is to find early examples of that individual's work to use as a base reference. I am not really a fan of comparison, but seeing where your idols started can be useful — and even more helpful if you discover they started in the shallow end of the talent pool.

This realization truly was an epiphany for me, empowering me to make far more attempts at things than I might have otherwise made. It also helped lead to my philosophy on trying.

My philosophy on trying is simple: *don't*. I know, I am starting to sound like Bart Simpson: "Can't win. Don't try." But in fact, I mean the exact opposite.

I talk about this idea a lot in my speaking gigs, and the advice holds true for this book. The main barrier to progress is not a lack of knowledge; it is a lack of *application* of that knowledge. And that is the reason that I have 100% decided to stop trying, and why I want you to stop trying as well.

Let's look at the definition of the word. "Try: an effort to accomplish something; an attempt."

In place of trying, what we need to do is start practicing.

Let's look again at the dictionary definition. "Practice: perform (an activity) or exercise (a skill) repeatedly or regularly in order to improve or maintain one's proficiency."

In other words, where "trying" privileges the end goal itself, "practicing" focuses on the process.

There are six fundamental reasons we should stop trying:

1. Our Language Shapes Us

The person with whom you communicate most is yourself. Like any interaction of communication, it is important that we precisely convey the message that we want to get across. The first step in this process with our internal dialogue is awareness. We need to be aware of what we are saying, so that we can make the decision whether or not to accept the language we are using or to use a different word to convey the message.

2. Giving up trying is easy

When we shift our language, we shift our focus. We are far more likely to continue practicing than we are to keep trying. Experiment by replacing the word "try" with the word "practice" in your internal dialogue.

3. Trying is stressful

Let's face it: when we try and accomplish something, we put a lot of pressure on ourselves to succeed. That can be tremendously stressful, and we risk not being content or satisfied with the work we are doing.

4. Trying leaves us open to failure

Trying implies a pass/fail outcome. We "try" something, and we are either successful or unsuccessful. The problem with this approach is that it leaves us an easy out. How many times have you heard this phrase? "Yeah, I tried that. It didn't work." We put a stop sign at the end of the attempt.

5. Shifting our focus to practice leads to improvement

By shifting our language from "try" to "practice," we change our expectations. We never fail at practice. Practice usually leads to improvement, no matter how marginal. Psychologically, this approach also allows us to come back and confidently repeat a task, with no expectation other than to improve on our last attempt.

6. Not trying gives us permission to attempt the unthinkable

Fear of failure often prevents people from even making an attempt. When we change our language, we open up our expectations to a myriad of variations which define success. This gives us the freedom to experiment, knowing that every attempt is simply a milestone toward whatever skill it is we are practicing.

Intentionally shifting my vocabulary from "trying" to "practicing" has allowed me to attempt and accomplish more than I ever have in the past. The fact of the matter is, if I had "tried" to write this book, you likely would not have it in your hand. I have simply "practiced" writing until I have reached a result that I feel good about sharing with you.

Another simple truth is, if I had not applied this concept to my dating life, I would not have ended up meeting the woman that would change everything.

WHEN SOMETHING'S GOTTA CHANGE:

What have you avoided "trying" that you might actually be able to "practice" in your life?

What would your life look like in six months from now if you practiced this simple word substitution? (see what I did there?)

CHAPTER 23

KARISSA

When I first saw Karissa online, I knew I was going to have to pull out my best ammunition. She was stunningly beautiful, with a profile clearly written by an extremely intelligent, grounded woman. I needed to come up with something that would grab her attention.

I took a risk and went with the subject line, "I think that's bullshit"— hoping that the swear would grab her and that curiosity would encourage her to read more. My message started by finishing the subject line with "...that a woman as beautiful and clearly intelligent as you is on a dating site." Well, apparently it worked. It worked very well, in fact.

She replied quickly and, after one or two exchanges, sent me her phone number so that we could communicate directly. Many of the women I had met online were hesitant to give up a phone number, so

I have to admit this contrast made me wonder about her.

I went back online to review her profile again, only to discover that it was gone. I was suspicious, as she definitely seemed a little too good to be true. I ended up googling her phone number; her photography website confirmed her identity and location in Fort Saskatchewan, as she'd told me. I felt a bit more comfortable, and after more conversation over text, we arranged to meet a few days later.

Later that night Karissa messaged me to say that she would actually be in Sherwood Park, where my office was, the next day and asked if I had any time available. I arranged to have her come by my office around lunch time. Lunch was a safe bet for both of us — a meal that needed to be eaten anyway and not so long as to be painful if there was absolutely no connection. I still had a little trepidation over how quickly this had all come together, still being somewhat naive to the whole online dating thing. We eventually signed off and said good night.

The next day at the office, it was all I could do to remain on task as I eagerly awaited my lunch date. I couldn't help but be tempted to put on a "facade" to impress this lovely woman. I ditched the idea as quickly as it came. I was 46 years old, and as Popeye would say, "I yam what I yam." Love me or hate me, she was getting the real deal.

Karissa showed up just before noon. When I saw her come in, I wasn't entirely certain what I felt. I'd love to tell you our eyes locked across the room and I knew instantly that she was the one. That didn't happen.

She was extremely attractive — slender, graceful long limbs, gorgeous long brown hair. She wore a flowing white skirt and had a tattoo with the word "Freedom" prominently featured in a henna pattern encircling her forearm. She was definitely stunning, although I remember looking at her and thinking, *OK, I think she's going to be a little too flower child or hippie for my taste.* You know, that whole "judge a book by its cover" thing.

It was a nice, warm spring day, so I suggested we walk across the street to have lunch at a nearby restaurant. She readily agreed. She had a quiet confidence and ease in her manner that I couldn't help but find appealing. She moved with the grace of a cat.

Karissa didn't say a lot on the walk over. She was soft spoken, yet with an air of *knowing*. I made some attempts to engage, to which she politely responded. Once we settled into the comfort of the restaurant, the conversation flowed smoothly. It became readily apparent that she was much more than the hippie flower child I had pegged her to be.

Karissa made it extremely easy to naturally be me. Although I had made the decision at the beginning of my dating journey that I would not put on pretence to impress a woman, that I would not be anything but true to who I was, being authentic was not always as easy as it sounds. But with Karissa it was effortless.

Immediately we slipped into deep, thought-provoking conversation. Both still a little bit shy and nervous, we sat in silence a few times when the conversation waned. Our eyes would meet, and the small smile that played at her lips — revealing her two front teeth and the small gap between them — let me know that this was anything but awkward silence. This was contentment, two individuals simply being in each other's presence without the need to force the words or rush the conversation. We talked about our kids (she had five ranging in age from 10 to 21), authors, podcasts, personal development, and personal philosophies.

I should be ashamed to admit I didn't expect such a deep intellect underneath that gorgeous hippie exterior. I was very pleasantly surprised. Karissa asked simple questions that challenged my way of thinking and shared lessons and quotes from favourite authors and podcasts. It wouldn't be until much later that I would fully realize the impact some of those details would have on my life.

I asked her about her philosophy on love. I shared with her some of my recent explorations and wonderings on the subject. "I am starting to be less convinced that there really is 'The One,'" I concluded. "Perhaps there's just '*The* Next One.' Maybe that's okay."

Karissa listened to my monologue on the subject, reflecting thoughtfully.

"I try to love with an open heart and open eyes," she said quietly.

It was here on our first date that she first blew my mind. I had likely spent ten minutes meandering around to make my point; she succinctly truncated her thoughts to those eleven words. We sat in silence again. It was honestly some of the most comfortable calm I have ever known: peace, contentment, lightness, calm — I struggle to articulate the feeling.

In hindsight, perhaps it was as simple as this: Karissa was being her, and I was being me.

"I try to love with an open heart and open eyes."

There was no expectation, no judgement, just acceptance and ease. I knew at that moment that this relationship was going to be special. I had no idea for sure where it would go, but I knew that this woman would become a very important part of my life.

Now that I think back, it was likely because we were both in a very similar spot on our journey to self-discovery and in our lives. We had both put in important work on ourselves and were finally becoming who we were supposed to be. We both had children and didn't want to start new families. I don't know if I am romanticizing in recollection, but when two souls who are on the same path connect at the same location on their journey, it creates a tremendous, powerful force, an energy that's hard to ignore. That's what happened that day.

Later that evening, we exchanged a few more texts, recapping some of the discussions that we had had over lunch. I was still extremely curious about this woman and what ran through her mind. I was eager to engage in further conversation and could not wait to see her again. We arranged a dinner date Thursday that week at a local restaurant.

I should back up a little bit, because a doctor's appointment the previous week would become extremely relevant to this story and how fast we were able to progress as a couple.

To recap where I was in life: I was 46 years old, just back on the dating scene, with two teenage children. It dawned on me early in the dating process that I still had a little work to do before dating was truly safe for me. I had no desire to expand my role as father, in starting fresh with a young family again, and I realized that I had important business before I moved forward in the dating scene. Enter the doctor and my appointment for a vasectomy. The fateful day was the Friday prior to meeting Karissa.

If you've been through the experience, you know how odd it can be. I am not going to paint a picture of the gentle martyr taking one for the greater good of mankind. To say it was a painful procedure would be a lie. I was honestly surprised at how effortless it was. But to say it was awkward would be an extreme understatement. There is something disconcerting about having a casual conversation about golf, sports, and other physical activities that you enjoy while another man holds your scrotum.

I had opted for the no-scalpel variation of the vasectomy, somewhat comforted that there would be no sharp blades anywhere near my penis. As much false bravado as I may put on about my manhood, this was really a big source of insecurity for me, so a doctor wielding a blade around such a literal and figuratively sensitive area really was a big deal.

I think the kicker was when he finished and asked me if I wanted to keep the severed pieces.

I gave him a look of astonishment and said, "Really?!"

"Some people keep them as a keepsake."

I quickly said, "No thanks," trying not to think of why you would actually want to keep a piece of your vas deferens on display anywhere. He handed me the post op instructions and left me alone to read them.

On my second date with Karissa, believe me, those instructions were floating around in my mind.

On Thursday, we met for dinner. Conversation was easy, she was beautiful, and I couldn't imagine things having gone any better. We had dinner, finished dessert, and drank about as much coffee as two people could reasonably handle late in the day. We sat there in silence, clearly enjoying each other's company and not wanting the evening to end. I think I stammered a lame, "So would you like to do something else?" It felt eerily reminiscent of Ralph Wiggim on *The Simpsons* when he approached Lisa Simpson on Valentine's Day with the classic line, "So...you...like stuff?"

Fortunately for me, the desire to keep the evening alive was mutual. We tossed around a couple of ideas that really did not go anywhere, and eventually she came up with the most brilliant idea ever. "I have my slackline in the truck. Would you like to go work the slackline?"

"Sure, that sounds great." Pause for dramatic effect. "Um... what the hell is a slackline?"

She laughed and went on to explain that slacklining refers to the act of walking or balancing along a suspended length of flat webbing tensioned between two anchors.

"All we need is two solid trees maybe 10 meters apart," she explained. "Do you know of any parks where we could find a setup like that?"

Now, I know most of you will question my motives, as I'm sure

Karissa must have. But I honestly could not think of a park where I could positively identify a couple of trees a reasonable distance apart. And I certainly wasn't interested in spending the evening driving around looking for an appropriate venue to slackline.

I thought of my house, close by on a huge lot in a mature neighbourhood with plenty of trees. I deliberated for a moment or two and, at the risk of sounding bold, said, "We could go back to my place. I have a huge yard with a lot of trees, several of which would be suitable for stringing up your slackline."

Much to my relief, Karissa did not seem to take umbrage at the suggestion and readily agreed. I suspect there might have been a little excited anticipation behind that quiet, contented smile she wore. We had met at the restaurant, so we agreed that she would follow me back to my place to set up the slackline.

After 15 years out of the dating scene, I had no moves.

I was pretty excited as I led the short drive back to the house. This would be an entirely new experience for me (the slackline, of course; stay focused). I had really learned to appreciate new experiences and definitely relished the opportunity for this one with my beautiful new friend. I had a slight bit of performance anxiety as we drove, and, yes, I am talking about the slacklining. But one of the most incredible things about this woman was that I was already certain Karissa would never judge anything I did. Although we had not had a lot of time together, it was an air that she gave off, and the trepidation passed quickly.

We arrived at my house, and after a quick tour, we headed to the backyard. We quickly found a couple of trees that would do the trick and set up her line stretching between them. The line hovered about three feet off the ground, giving me a little comfort: a spill would not likely break my neck. More likely a rolled ankle and a bruised ego. That I could handle.

Karissa jumped on the line and started to balance, her limbs long and her brown hair flowing in the warmth of the late spring sun, complemented by the smell of pine trees and the illusion of isolation the tree-lined yard provided. In the words of Don Henley, I get a peaceful, easy feeling just thinking of her balancing on that line, walking first one way, holding her balance, lunging and turning around to come back the other way. I was as excited as I was terrified for my turn. As accepting as she was, it was still going to take a bit for me to swallow my pride, realizing that I would have nowhere near the skill or grace that she possessed.

My turn came and I put one foot on the line, knee bent, ready to stand and balance. My first objective was just to stand on the line. When I shifted my weight off my grounded foot and started to slide it over to the line, I was astonished by how my leg shook. It looked like I was standing on a jackhammer. I placed my weight back on the grounded foot, putting a stop to the vibration. Regroup, retry. Same thing! No matter what I did, I could not get my leg to stop vibrating.

After probably a dozen tries, my body sweating profusely, my leg finally started to respond to my will to stand fast. I was eventually able to pop up on one foot, balancing on the line. First for a second, then for two, but not much more than that. I was amazed at how physically demanding the feat was. I was exhausted.

Karissa walked over and climbed onto our nearby trampoline. She bounced higher and higher, making eye contact, her smile inviting me to join her. We bounced together for a while and eventually sat, legs splayed, facing each other on the trampoline, the verbal banter between us slowly diminishing as our connected gaze intensified. There was a palpable energy between us.

I'm not sure how long we sat there together, but it became clear that it was time for me to make a move.

I failed miserably. I. Had. No. Moves.

Fortunately, Karissa was a woman of action. She leaned over, touching my shins, shook her hair clear of her face, and said, "Are you going to kiss me or what?"

I may be a little slow in the moves department, but I certainly wasn't going to let an invitation like that slide. I shuffled forward, touched her face with my fingertips, gazed into her eyes, paused to drink her in, then leaned in for a kiss.

No doubt there was a connection between us.

We started softly. My hand slid gently down her cheek, pushing her hair back and eventually coming to rest on the back of her neck, softly stroking her hair. She began to kiss me more vigorously, mouth wide. Our tongues connecting, I pulled her hard toward me. The sounds of our breathing became more frantic as we absorbed as much of each other as we possibly could.

After a few minutes, coming up for air, she looked at me and breathlessly said, "Inside?"

I nodded, took her hand, and led her inside. We went straight to the family room and climbed into my two-person nest chair, perfect for just such an occasion.

As our make-out session escalated, I realized that I was going to have to put the brakes on. I was not in a position to take this to its logical outcome. I slowed things down and explained about the vasectomy. Once again, nothing but acceptance and understanding from Karissa. I felt disappointed, yet I was somewhat relieved that my performance anxiety wouldn't rear its ugly head for a second time that evening.

From the start, I could be myself with Karissa, even if that meant showing a vulnerable or even embarrassing side to myself. It was a huge relief, especially in comparison to the experiences I had had previously.

After three years of self-reflection, focusing on who I wanted to be, I had been hopeful I would finally find someone who would be the right connection for me, someone who would round out the life that I had built. Someone who would not only enhance my life but, maybe more importantly, I theirs. And now, here she was.

When you put in the work, good things come. While I craved the connection and love from a partner, I wasn't prepared to sacrifice who I had become in the process. In my early years, I focused so much on what I *thought* I wanted that I was trying to project the type of person whom I imagined would get those things. I spent far too much time pretending to be someone I believed I needed to be, and nowhere near enough time discovering who I actually was. Now, I was far beyond putting on a facade for anyone.

Sometimes it's much less about becoming who you want to be and more about realizing who you already are.

That realization is never as easy as it sounds. The hardest — and best — thing you can ever do is take a good, honest look at yourself in the mirror and simply accept, without judgement, the person staring back at you. Amazing things start to happen when we let the person we are rise to the surface, when we stop suppressing who we really are in the misguided desire to be something different.

Learning to live comfortably in your own skin can be incredibly challenging. We are inundated with societal messages designed to convince us that we are not enough the way we are. If only we have this product or that service, we will somehow be more fulfilled. Billions of dollars are spent every year researching how to ensure we feel inadequate, and billions more spent to share those messages. Marketers employ doctorate-level psychology to guarantee that we know that we are "not enough" as we are. *But wait! There's more! For three easy payments you, too, can have the latest gimmick to fill your self-*

worth bucket!

The problem is, as I suspect you know, that the bucket always empties again, and we start looking for the next thing to fill it.

We are constantly in a fight with our own self-image in the pursuit of worthiness.

It was almost two years before Karissa — and a year after my separation — that the concept of *becoming* really hit home with me. I had just delivered the opening keynote at Axiom Mortgage's national conference down in New Orleans. In the audience were some long-time industry friends, many of whom had watched my evolution both as a businessman and a human being. Among them was Renee, who over the years had become not only a colleague but also a very good friend, someone I knew I could trust when the chips were down. She was one of the first mortgage associates to join my fledgling company in the early years. She had had a front row seat for ten years of the Evolution of Mike. I was incredibly moved when, after that day at the conference, she came up to me with her signature smile, gave me a great big hug, and said, "I think you are finally becoming who you are supposed to be."

I think you are finally becoming who you are supposed to be.

Renee's comment will stay with me for a lifetime. And that's when I truly started to realize that no matter what you do in life, no matter how you feel you measure up, the only true measure of success is how true you are being to yourself.

Enter Karissa.

Because only when we are our most authentic do we attract the people in our lives who we truly want to be with. While this fact may not have been abundantly clear at the time I met her, it certainly is now: Karissa was a gift to me for the years of work I had put into myself. I in no way mean to make it sound like she was a possession, or a prize. The reality is, we had both done a lot of hard self-work and were equally blessed to have finally found each other. Unexpected though it may have been, the work I had put in was certainly producing results far beyond what I would have ever imagined.

Unfortunately, I did not fully appreciate the enormity of what was happening at the time. These are the moments we need to stop and take note of, to spend time observing and appreciating as they happen. Make no mistake, I thoroughly enjoyed the relationship developing between us, but I'm not sure I fully appreciated it as much as I could have in the moment. Another reminder to practice gratitude in our lives.

It's easy to ignore or downplay the positives as we chalk up negativity on the scorecard in our minds. When I'm surrounded by a plethora of events that are not necessarily positive, I have to remind myself to acknowledge the amazing things going on.

I can hear it now: "Yeah, Mike, you think you've got it tough? Well, let me tell you...." But no matter what's going on in your own life right now, and as much as I'm sure some aspects of life suck, I am also equally certain you have many things for which to be grateful.

We all get caught up in the need to justify our misery, forgetting the blessings that we've been given. This is why it's so important to practice gratitude regularly, not an easy thing to do. We have a choice. We can choose to dwell on the shit hand we have been dealt, or we can shift our focus and choose to be grateful for moments we have right now.

I would not likely have admitted it in those early days, but I was still mired in the lingering resentment of past failed relationships. As much as I enjoyed the "us" of it, I was reluctant to put too much focus on the here and now, instead living in the past. I also worried about the future. While I was definitely concerned about getting hurt again, my greater fear was having someone put themselves in a position where I could break their heart. I was far more adept at handling my own sorrow than I was with the possibility of causing someone else any measure of grief.

I could justify not being fully engaged. My "rational" mind deluded me into believing that I was protecting both of us from potential heartbreak. The reality of what I was doing was robbing us of moments of time that we will never get back. It wasn't altruistic, it was selfish — and an incredible waste.

Granted, at the beginning of relationships, we should exercise a modicum of caution. But who are we if we are not fully investing in any of the relationships we are in? For fear of rejection, hurt, or maybe even fear of happiness, we cover ourselves in heavy cloaks of chain mail, never allowing ourselves to be fully *seen*. It is easier for us to take the safe route, to not fully show up.

Our lens of inadequacy usually prevents us from being authentic. We wear masks even in our closest relationships. We are quick to decide that once our partners or friends see the real us, they will also see the same inadequacies that we see in ourselves.

As much progress as I had made, I still had numerous lessons to learn in the art of being present.

WHEN SOMETHING'S GOTTA CHANGE:

It really is amazing what happens when we can become comfortable in our own skin. When we make the daily decision to simply show up as we truly are without fear of judgement.

How would you act and speak if you were to be entirely true to who you are?

____

____

____

____

What is preventing you from doing that?

____

____

____

____

CHAPTER 24

PATIENCE AND PRESENCE

One of the earliest things that Karissa taught me was the practice of presence and how to see the world through the eyes of an artist. She was an exceptional photographer, painter, and videographer and viewed the world through an artistic lens. She would often stop and point out the scene that was unfolding in front of us, whether that was a bird flitting by as we were out on a walk or the rustle of the trees as the wind blew through. You could see her composing images in her mind as she stopped and became immersed in our surroundings.

The depth of Karissa's ability to focus on the present moment was never more apparent than the evening we went to see the Edmonton Symphony Orchestra. As the music started, it was evident that it completely enveloped her. I was fascinated. I remember watching her absorb every last note the orchestra played. I could imagine her feeling each and every instrument as they came together to weave the beautiful melodies of Bach.

While I was never talented in the musical or visual arts, I enjoyed writing and soon realized I could take a page out of Karissa's book to practice the art of being fully present. I had recently read *On Writing* by Stephen King where he talks about the real power of writing. King says that in order to write well, you must first observe well. I decided to employ this as a strategy whenever the thought crossed my mind. I would look for opportunities to write the scene in my head as it was unfolding in front of me. If I practiced writing what was happening, then I had to notice all the little nuances, thereby becoming fully present and aware.

An example of my newfound awareness came while out on a long ride with my triathlon club. It was a chilly Sunday morning. We met at a high school parking lot. At sunrise, there were no cars in the lot other than those of the teammates who would be joining us for the long training ride.

As my fellow triathletes started to arrive, unload bikes, and prepare their gear, I could hear the variety of conversations playing out on an otherwise quiet morning. I Inhaled the aroma of the McCafe box of coffee that Shawn so thoughtfully brought to share with the group before we set off. The palpable chill of the fresh northern Alberta morning, the scene some 20KM in — unfolding as a red-headed woodpecker, rustled from his perch in the nearby brush, flew out, paced us briefly, then flitted off into the horizon. Writing out the scene in my head as it blossomed in reality certainly allowed for a much more vibrant ride than I might have otherwise achieved.

Being present was only one of the many gifts Karissa shared with me in the early days of our relationship.

Karissa and I started spending more and more time together. She very quickly became my best friend, something that might sound cliché if it hadn't been so true. Not that we weren't romantically involved right from the beginning, but our relationship was absolutely rooted in a deep friendship, so much so that at times I wondered if we were destined to only be friends.

And then I fell in love with her.

Karissa was the first woman who ever became my best friend first and my love second. It was an epiphany for me: almost all of my previous relationships had begun with some sort of infatuation or love interest out of the gate. From there, we always tried to force a friendship.

Even after this revelation, I was still a little bit emotionally guarded. I had my walls up after my last relationship, and once again I had begun wondering about the validity of love itself. Karissa would call me out on this attitude every so often. In hindsight, it really was a disrespectful thing to do to her.

Sky Diving

I realize now how patient she was with me, absolutely giving me my space to figure things out and not placing any pressure on our relationship at all. Leading by example, Karissa taught me patience, something with which I have long struggled. I was always hesitant to make plans in advance and tended to operate last minute, partly because that's my nature, but there was also an element of a fear of commitment in there as well. If you are a planner at heart and have a partner who is more the spontaneous sort, you likely are shaking your head in frustration. Certainly, this part of my personality used to drive Christine absolutely batty — which is why I so greatly appreciated Karissa's patience with me.

One particular morning, we texted first thing with our traditional good morning greetings and asked about each other's day. Karissa had told me she had a video shoot downtown at 1 p.m. and not much else planned for the day. As I headed into the office, I thought about connecting with her later that day, possibly skipping out a little early to do so.

I meant to message her first thing with my idea and set something up, but as usual when I hit the office, I was inundated with things to do, time getting away on me. Before I knew it, it was 11 a.m. and I still had not messaged her.

I picked up my phone and sent her a note asking if she might be interested in stopping for a coffee or drink on her way home from downtown. She replied that she wasn't sure she'd be able to. I was a little perplexed because she had indicated she didn't have any plans. I asked what was up, heart in throat, mind leaping to all the reasons she may not want to spend time with me.

"Well, if I can get this shoot done in a reasonable amount of time and can get out to Eden North by 5 o'clock, I'm going to go jump out of an airplane."

We had discussed doing a jump together, so I was a little surprised.

"Who are you going with?" I texted back, my jealousy hackles up a little.

"I'm going on my own."

Karissa had decided that morning to check availability, and it just so happened they had a spot open that afternoon.

"Wait! What? You're jumping without me?"

"Dude, I can hardly get a coffee commitment out of you. I'm not waiting around for you!"

For about two seconds, I felt something akin to anger or resentment. We had planned to go together!

And then my heart swelled with pride. This was my kind of woman. She wasn't going to take any of my bullshit. She wasn't about to let my commitment issues hold her back from doing what she loved to do. I admired that in her immensely.

Karissa seemed like the perfect woman for me.

WHEN SOMETHING'S GOTTA CHANGE:

How we show up in our relationships has a massive role in the success or failure of those relationships.

What walls do you put up to appear tough or to protect yourself from getting hurt?

____

____

____

____

How would your relationships improve if you were less guarded?

____

____

____

____

CHAPTER 25

CLIMB LIKE A GIRL

In August of 2015, Karissa and I took a road trip to Penticton, BC. Penticton is a small summer town located in South Central British Columbia, an area known as the Okanagan some 250 miles east of Vancouver. When I was a kid growing up, we vacationed there almost every year. I remember joining the throngs of summer tourists that would float down the 4-mile long river channel that connected the two lakes flanking the city to the North and South. Some of my fondest memories include fishing for bullheads off the campground pier and then heading to the local ice cream shop for some Tiger Tail ice cream.

This year we were there for the 2015 Challenge Penticton half-iron distance triathlon. You see, I had done the Calgary Ironman 70.3 in July, and I decided since I was already trained up, I might as well do the Penticton race. I had lived in the city for a summer with my Aunt Sharon, Uncle Jerry, and cousins Susan and Lynn, when I was in my early teens. The town has always had a special place in my heart.

Although the main purpose of the trip was the triathlon, Karissa had a passion for climbing, and I had asked her to look into climbs in the area. It turns out that Skaha Bluffs, just 15 minutes outside of the city, offered some spectacular climbing.

We only had one extra day in Penticton, the day after my race. My first outdoor climbing experience would come directly on the heels of competing in a six-hour half-iron distance triathlon. This made me a little bit nervous, but it was important for me to give Karissa her chance to get in some climbing, so I decided I would suck it up and just make it happen.

Monday morning after my race, we headed off for Skaha Bluffs, and despite some teasing from Karissa to the contrary, I didn't feel very badass. I could hardly walk, let alone climb 20- to 40-metre cliffs. I let Karissa know that I might have to just belay her — that is, tend the rope while she climbed.

My mother and aunt, who had come out to cheer me on for the triathlon, decided to come along and watch the beginning of our climb and carry on for a walk of their own.

It was an absolutely magical day. I had that nervous excitement that you get when you are a) in love and b) about to try something new for the first time. Karissa had her trademark little smile playing at her lips that let me know she was extremely grateful we were able to enjoy this together. She was also excited about the prospect of climbing outdoors, something she had not yet done on Canadian soil.

We parked at the trailhead to the bluffs and walked together hand in hand on the pathway behind my mother and Sharon. Walking with my mother is more like a sprint than a walk. She's usually a few hundred metres ahead of everyone else. This day was no exception. Fortunately, Mom paused to take a photo of Karissa and me together, walking down the hill, hand in hand, capturing one of my favourite moments with this incredible woman.

Not long after this photo was taken, we found a spot at the base of one of the many options of rock wall. Mom and Sharon carried on to finish their hike and head back to town. Consulting the guidebook Karissa had brought, we settled at the base of an easy 20+ metre climb. I took a minute to survey the landscape, noting the variety of crags and other climbers enjoying the day. A view of a climber on a distant face some 50+ metres up in the air sent my heart to my throat. Was I really ready for this? Taking a moment, I took a breath as we settled in, strapped on our gear, and performed our gear check ritual. One of these checks was a quick tug on the gear loops of the harness to make sure that the harness was tight enough and would not fall down over the hips of the climber. Karissa added an extra step of her own. She yanked down on my loops, pulled my hips into hers, and leaned in to give me a quick kiss. It became a fun little tradition that we continued to follow every time that we climbed.

That day at the Bluffs, long after Mom and Aunt Sharon had gone back, Karissa and I stayed, exploring a variety of faces, crags, and routes, enjoying each other's company in the solitude of the hills, well into the evening.

That day would become one of my favourite memories with Karissa.

Ease Over Effort

Climbing is largely a partner sport, and you have to be comfortable with your partner's setup before you allow them to climb with you, belay them, or belay you. When Karissa first took me to the climbing gym where she practiced, I was not skilled or experienced enough to belay her, but we still went through the rituals of checking each other's gear.

Those first few times at the gym were frustrating for me. She moved so gracefully and effortlessly on that wall, while I clenched, stressed, and bumbled my way around. Her patience was incredibly soothing. She would often encourage me to take a break, when all I wanted to do was get back up and conquer that wall. Her peacefulness was contagious. I soon found myself relaxing more into the climb and following her lead, slowing things down, moving more deliberately than forcefully. I was and still am a long way away from her skill level, but the lesson was strong, and one I continue to learn and one whose importance I realize more and more each day.

Sometimes you can accomplish more with ease than with power.

This concept seems incredibly counterintuitive. After all, our entire lives we have been taught to work hard and good things will come. As a highly driven person who has always taken immense pride in how hard he works, "ease over effort" does not come naturally for me. The journey to acceptance of this truism has been a long one for me. I was first introduced to the concept in running, then yoga, and then climbing. And learning to apply this physical realm notion to my mental wellbeing has been a game changer for me.

Growing up in Canada and playing hockey, I often heard the term "gripping the stick too tight." Professional hockey commentators and coaches alike use the phrase all the time, referring to a player who is tense and who makes mistakes that they might not otherwise. The skills are there from years of practice, yet on any given day the pressure can catch up to even the most talented players.

When it comes to running, it may have been my triathlon coach Dan who first told me, "Sometimes to run faster, you have to run slower." What was he talking about? I didn't understand; in my world if you wanted to run faster... you ran faster. The logical, Spock-like part of my brain strongly resisted this concept. The current push to higher intensity, lower duration workouts as a magic workout for almost everything — Crossfit is a great example of a regimen that proselytizes high intensity — was a philosophy I loved

Sometimes you have to run slow to run faster.

and could understand.

So when Coach Dan prescribed my long runs at a 7:00 min/km pace, I almost choked. "You're shitting me!" I sputtered. To put this pace in perspective, my race time for a half marathon at the time was closer to 5:00 min/km, so reducing that pace by 40% seemed excessive. Fortunately, I am very coachable and always willing to experiment. As I would later learn, recent evidence suggests that running slower for the majority of your workouts has significant benefits, not the least of which is less injury, and allows you to crank up the mileage with less risk.

The net result? A faster time come race day. Who knew?

When it came to yoga, it was a little easier to wrap my head around the idea of "ease." After all, yoga is all about slowing down, the primary reason I practiced it. I still struggled with the idea of easing into some of those more complex poses. I worked on maintaining a solid headstand in yoga for a long time. I worked my core, strengthening all the muscle groups required to hold the pose, and worked my ass off to make that sucker happen. So many components make up the pose: the alignment of arms, head, chest, the engagement of your core and shoulder muscles. All those parts work hard to support those tootsies floating way up in the sky where your head is supposed to be.

While I had started slowly having a modicum of success with the inversion, I still assumed I really had to work hard for it. The more I thought about the headstand, the harder I worked, the less success I found. It was only when I started to let go of the mechanics of it and eased in, trusting the process and the practice, that the pose would start to come for me. In fact, I found the best headstands came when I did not take the time to set them up in my mind ahead of time and simply let my intuitive self guide my body into the pose.

In short, I could accomplish much more with practice and ease than with sheer effort.

When it came to climbing, this phenomenon was even more pronounced. I laugh now and to this day I can hear Karissa's frequent encouragement, even when I am bouldering alone: "Climb like a girl! Climb like a girl!"

As a man I tend to like to "power" through things. I think I have a tendency to believe that if I am strong enough, I can accomplish anything. I am officially calling bullshit on this expectation, particularly for men. Now, I do not want to take away from the amazing male climbers out there, but my experience observing both genders at the gym reveals that women are often much more graceful and adept at climbing.

Climbing is not a sport you can muscle your way through for any great length of time. While you may be able to power through a move or two, before long your muscles become fatigued and you become "pumped out.' Once your arms are cooked, you're done.

Climbing is a sport of finesse even more than strength. For many of us self-motivated, driven individuals, we believe that we can do anything if we simply apply more effort. In climbing this is rarely the case. When I would try and muscle my way up the wall, arms perpetually bent, using all the effort I had to pull myself up, Karissa would yell from below, "Climb like a girl! Climb like a girl!" as a reminder to ease into it, to straighten my arms and move with more grace than force.

Watching Karissa climb was a joy. She moved with such lightness, every move looking effortless, like water flowing uphill.

Climbing for me has become an outlet similar to yoga. Both focus on that forced presence of being, that mindful awareness of your surroundings. When you're on the rock wall, whether indoor or outdoor, you need to be focused on your next move. While you plan your route and see the big picture, when you're on the wall, the only thing on the planet is that 4 x 8 foot section of rock or wall in front of you. If you don't want to fall, you need to be 100% in the moment and focused on exactly what you're doing. The sport is physically demanding for certain, but climbing is really about finding the integration of effort and ease that makes for a good ascent. Today, I climb regularly with a guide, and the sport continues to challenge me and instruct me in life as much as in physical agility and strength.

Grotto Falls

Although I'd already been ice climbing for a few years, I recently did my first lead at Grotto Falls under the tutelage of my friend Margo. Up until this point, I'd only followed people up frozen waterfalls, but on this day, I would be the one to put the rope up, putting in screws for protection as I went.

Grotto Falls is located in a picturesque canyon approximately one hour east of the world-famous Banff, Alberta. The sun was shining as we hiked the thirty-minute approach to the climb, passing beneath the slot canyon's rock walls that at times revealed ancient pictographs from a bygone era.

The canyon trail eventually opens up to a large rock face that in winter is host to two ice seeps that stand 15 metres tall and an equal distance apart. The two pillars of ice, called "His" and "Hers," commanded attention, because while they were shorter than our objective, they were also much more difficult than I was prepared to lead that day. A short, ice-covered gully to the right of these seeps led us to our final destination, Grotto Falls. The route is 60 metres in length, at a relatively easy grade. In other words: perfect for a first lead. The climb is typically done in two sections, or 'pitches,' splitting the falls in half.

Here again, I experienced the concept of ease over effort in spades. Over the past few years of ice climbing I have always "top roped," where someone better than me has gone ahead and led the climb to set up a rope up top. When you are top roping, you are always secured by a rope fastened above you. There is very little danger if the rope is properly set, as the person belaying you can keep the rope tight, leaving very little margin for a fall.

In contrast, when you lead, you are always placing your own protection as you go. This means that the rope is always fastened to the ice below you. If you climb ten feet above your last piece of protection (an ice screw) and fall, you are falling the ten feet of slack you have brought up with you *plus* the ten feet below your protection until the rope catches. The consequences for falling are substantially greater, putting a much higher degree of stress on lead climbing versus top roping.

I would be leading the second pitch, meaning I got to follow on the first climb for a warm up. That first climb that day, I was nervous and gripping my tools extremely tight. My calves were over-engaged, and I was using as much effort as I could to power my way up that frozen waterfall. When I got to the anchor station, I was drained. This was not a good sign; this was a relatively easy climb, and it would now be my turn to lead.

I recognized quickly that in order to be successful on this lead, I would need to ease into the climb and not use effort. That second climb was one of the most pronounced applications of this concept I have ever experienced. I was nervous to begin with — to be frank, I was *fucking terrified* — so it took everything I had not use as much effort as possible.

As I try to explain my experience, I realize again how counterintuitive "ease over effort" seems.

As I made my way up the ice and noticed I was gripping too tightly or kicking too hard on easy ice, I made the conscious decision to relax into it. The difference was immediate. When I slowed down, trusted my training, and moved with the grace that mentors like Karissa had shown me, everything became more effortless by an order of magnitude. I relaxed my grip on my ice tools, trusted my feet, and focused on placing my next screw. Practice, rehearse, repeat all the way to the top of the pitch, where I had the opportunity to build my first anchor that would be used to belay my mentor below up to join me.

I had an incredible sense of accomplishment once we got back down. While not all of the movements were smooth and graceful, I can certainly recall the moments where I allowed myself to melt into ease. I also know that these moments of grace and ease, while fleeting on that first lead, will start to string together more frequently, until eventually my entire climb becomes a picture of fluid agility.

Ease Into Life

What becomes even more important than applying this concept in our chosen sports is learning how to apply this approach to all aspects of our lives. This is really just another iteration of the concept of "Embrace the Suck." When it comes to our emotional challenges and pursuits, we can make substantially more progress with ease than we can with effort. If you are a Trekkie, you may be thinking of the phrase "resistance is futile." In the context of life and emotion, I am going to substitute the word "ease" for "surrender," as I think the latter is a more appropriate description.

We have a propensity to fight the bad feelings, hoping to replace them with good feelings. This rarely works out well. We cannot successfully combat negative emotions. They are not a dragon that needs to be slayed. First and foremost, there cannot be good feelings without the bad ones, just as there can be no "up" without "down" or "light" without "dark." You cannot have courage without fear. There can be no faith without doubt.

Secondly, you cannot pick and choose which feelings you get to experience. In other words, you cannot decide to feel the good and suppress or block out the bad. Emotion doesn't work that way. No amount of effort will allow us to 'send' our negative emotions.

Allowing ourselves to surrender into even the most difficult feelings is the most effective way of allowing them to dissipate.

I still had a lot to learn when it came to living with ease. My next lesson came from a very unlikely source.

WHEN SOMETHING'S GOTTA CHANGE:

The art of letting go and trusting the process is an incredibly difficult thing to do. I have found some amazing results when I am able to slow down and let ease overcome effort.

In what areas of your life are you "gripping the stick" too tightly?

____

____

____

____

What would it look like if you could swap effort for ease?

____

____

____

____

CHAPTER 26

REDEFINING BADASS

At some point early in our relationship Karissa started teasing me about how "badass" I was. She loved that I embraced new challenges and did things that scared the shit out of me. Ironman, yoga, climbing, Crossfit, and running a business were all things she deemed worthy of the title. I suspect she knew how much I secretly relished the nickname. As a guy who had always felt more geek than jock, more nerd than cool kid, my heart would swell with pride whenever she said it.

That night after our climb at the Skaha Bluffs, Aunt Sharon had Karissa, my mother, and me over for dinner. It was during our dinner conversation that I realized how *un*badass I was

Sharon is a proud Pentictonite who is active in the community. She had recently started doing small triathlons and was always looking to improve. In the lead-up to the full Challenge Penticton iron-distance triathlon, there are a number of events, including a 5km fun run. Sharon shared with us the story of how that race went for her.

"I knew full well I would be last, so I started at the back of the group of 60 or so participants."

This is where my reality check on my own "badass" status came into play. Finishing, even an iron distance race, in the middle of the pack is easy. It doesn't take a special kind of skill or courage. You actually cross the line quite inconspicuously and can proudly state that you competed and completed.

What does take courage, however, is to enter a race knowing perfectly well that you will be crossing the finish line dead last, with all eyes on you.

Aunt Sharon said that, with about one and a half kilometres left in the race, a young man named Lorne started pacing her on a bike. Sharon looked over her shoulder and said, "You're here because I'm last, aren't you?"

He answered, "I'm afraid so" — pause — "but you're doing great!"

Lorne continued to encourage her along, and when Sharon was within a few blocks of the finish line, he said he was going to ride ahead and let them know she was coming in. He rode off.

As she got within a few hundred metres of the finish line, Sharon said she could see that they had already pulled down the P.A. system, had lowered the finish line, and had started dismantling the announcer tables. But when Lorne came in and told them Sharon was still out on the course, everyone scrambled to set everything back up so they could announce her in.

They also sent an athlete out to run the final few hundred metres with her. The individual who joined her is a local professional triathlete named Jeff Symonds, winner of the 2013 Challenge Penticton full iron distance race and the 2015 Ironman Melbourne race. A pretty nice touch to keep her spirits up as she crossed the finish line.

When Sharon finished the story and got up to clear the table,

Karissa and I looked at each other with knowing gazes and wry smiles. Karissa leaned over and said, "Now that, my friend, is fucking badass!"

The strength, tenacity, and courage it took for Sharon to complete that 5km race puts a whole different shine on the word. Chuck Norris may claim the title, but he's got nothing on a 65-year-old woman who is determined to improve herself even at the risk of finishing dead last. The vulnerability involved in that endeavour is massive and not a situation most of our stereotypical badasses would put themselves in.

Aunt Sharon's experience got me thinking pretty hard about what it means to be a badass. The more I thought about it, the more I liked the handle. In fact, it was a word I was beginning to fold into the talks — a natural offshoot of my podcasts — I had recently started giving. From a presentation branding standpoint, the word stands out. Admit it or not, we all want to be a little more badass. I decided to look up the definition online. According to Google, the word means "a tough, uncompromising, or intimidating person."

So how do I reconcile the inner nerd with my new-found desire to be badass? I have always been one who has been fairly comfortable with his tender side. I do not always feel the need to live up to the stereotypical, societal version of "manly." In fact, trying to live up to that stereotype can be quite dangerous.

Trying to live up to the stereotypical definition of badass can be quite dangerous.

The premise is that if we accept the typical view that men should suppress their feelings, we also force men to become less emotionally intelligent, which can negatively affect our behaviours. As a guy who has studied the impact that emotion has on human behaviour for over twenty years in the context of sales and leadership, I can assure you that this is a very real problem. I've studied the likes of Dan Goleman,

Dr. Travis Bradbury and Dr. Antonio Demasio, to name a few. Dr. Demasio in particular has some very specific research supporting the fact that decisions are based on emotion first.

So how does this relate to being a badass? Well, again, the societal norm for men in particular is one that does not allow us to show a lot of emotion, one that expects us to put on a hard outer shell. This definition did not bode well for me being a badass. But it doesn't bode well for the men who do live up to that expectation, either.

On our ten-hour drive back from Penticton to Edmonton, Karissa and I discussed what it means to be "badass" in great detail. On that same trip, we were listening to Brene Brown talk about vulnerability on the Tim Ferriss show. Tim asked Brene about the perceived notion of the "over-feminization" of boys these days. The question caught me a little off guard, but Brene handled it brilliantly. She talked about masculine and feminine not being mutually exclusive. Then she said something that brought it all together for me, though I'm paraphrasing: "To me, the co-existence of tough and tender is the equation for baddassery."

Boom! Right on the money!

In short, we need the world to embrace the notion of redefining the word "badass," especially when it comes to men.

The bottom line is that the way men think about strong is wrong. For most of our lives, men have constantly been told to "man up," to "grow a set," or to "suck it up." The unfortunate consequence of such statements is that most men believe we should bury or suppress our emotions. As a result, we learn from a very early age to suppress, hide, or bottle up our "sensitive" side. We hide our emotions from the world for fear of becoming vulnerable and being seen as less of a man.

True strength isn't about avoiding, suppressing, or remaining stoic in the face of our emotions. True strength is having the courage to sit with our feelings, to observe and learn from them what we can.

As we moved out of childhood into our young adulthood and, eventually, the adult phase of our lives, how many times did we men hear or use the phrase "Suck it up, Princess," mocking those around us who let themselves become emotionally vulnerable? Men are constantly reminded by society that it is not "cool" or "manly" to be emotional, or to share our emotions, if we even admit to having them. Rarely will you hear men confide in each other about what they are feeling.

As I write this now, I can almost hear the ribbing from my male friends. Any time a man displays any emotional characteristics, he will surely be chastised by his male peers.

Little did I know how personal this concept would become to me, just a short month and a half later.

WHEN SOMETHING'S GOTTA CHANGE:

The societal pressure to put on the tough guy mask is strong, especially for men. It is important to slow down, open up, accept what is coming, and reconnect with our emotional selves.

What do you believe it means to be a "badass"?

____

____

____

____

Do you inadvertently put unrealistic pressure on the people in your life to live up to the stereotypical definition of badass?

____

____

____

____

CHAPTER 27

TELL ME I LOOK PRETTY

I had just published my 37th podcast episode. I had interviewed a fellow by the name of Bob Burg, who is the co-author of a book titled *The Go-Giver*.

I greeted Karissa at the door with a kiss. We debated spending some time on the slackline out back before eating. It was a mild fall evening: temperatures comfortably in the low teens Celsius, leaves close to turning, that autumn smell in the air. It was the kind of mood that would summon one to play the Eagles' "Peaceful Easy Feeling." In the end, I suggested that we head to a local restaurant/bar for a bite to eat and a drink, so we could review what I had learned on the podcast interview that day.

Have you ever had one of those days where you feel so light you just feel like skipping everywhere you go? Where each detail is embedded in your memory? That is how I felt that evening.

Karissa and I hopped in my Toyota Highlander and made the seven-minute drive to the restaurant. The sense of being fully present that this woman exuded was incredible. Nothing else but the moment at hand seemed to matter, though our optimism for a bright future was palpable.

After we were seated, I ordered a beer and she a martini. The conversation flowed effortlessly, as always, as we debated and challenged points made and lessons learned in my interview. When she ordered a second martini, I looked at her and said, "Oh, I'm in trouble tonight, aren't I?"

Karissa smiled her wry smile and gave me a look I recognized well: pure contentment.

At some point during the meal, I joked that I should interview her for my podcast, as she was a successful entrepreneur running her own photography business on top of managing to raise five children. She laughed with an ease that was only hers, leaning back, arms wide in invitation. "Bring it, Cameron!" she said.

So I did. I opened with the standard, "Who are you and what do you do?" She described herself as an artist, a yogi, a mother, and photographer. When I asked her why she went into business for herself, she explained that it was a matter of necessity, being a single mom of five kids. We laughed and then I asked her what she thought was the key to becoming a successful entrepreneur. Her response was some of the most straightforward, most profound advice I have heard, simple and elegant: "You have to keep your eye open for opportunity, and then seize it when it presents itself."

She went on to tell the story of her first job following her return to Canada, after living in LA for ten years with her ex-husband. She had gone into a day spa to buy a gift certificate for a loved one's birthday. The proprietor apologetically handed her a homemade brochure to accompany the gift certificate. She immediately recognized an opportunity to sell her graphic design skills and offered to create a proper brochure for the spa. Long story short, the owner accepted the offer, and just like that Karissa was in business for herself.

Oh, how I wish now that I had had my recording gear with me.

We wrapped up dinner and the mock interview. We had planned a nice quiet evening together, and she had come prepared to spend the night like she did many times when I didn't have my kids at home. Eventually we headed back to my place, curling up on the nest chair to read. She had a copy of *The Go-Giver* in her hand, and I a book on writing.

After about half an hour of reading, she closed the book and looked over at me with her quiet smile playing at her lips and shimmering in her eyes. I put my book down and met her gaze.

Referring to the first chapter of the book, Karissa said to me, "Hey, I've got a tip for you on adding value."

"Oh yeah? What's that?"

"When you think I look pretty, you should tell me."

I chuckled and said, "Well, of course you look pretty. You are gorgeous, and I always think that." My playful side kicked in. "I'll tell you what. How about if I think you look ugly, I will let you know. Otherwise, you can just assume that I think you look pretty."

As you can imagine, my flippant suggestion did not go over well. We ended up having a beautiful conversation about the importance of sharing how we see one another, which lasted well into the night. When you can start to see yourself through the eyes of someone who loves you, your world will never be the same.

The night was just an incredibly beautiful reminder to actively share how you feel about your loved ones — and my memory of the evening would go on to shape one of the most powerful lessons I would ever learn.

WHEN SOMETHING'S GOTTA CHANGE:

This may be the easiest section I have ever had to write. These are not questions; they are strong suggestions.

Connect with someone you love and tell them what they mean to you. Take a moment and write down who those people are.

____

____

____

____

Connect with someone who has made an impact on your life and let them know how they have touched you. Take a moment and write down who those people are.

____

____

____

____

CHAPTER 28

I remember hearing the alarm go off at 5 a.m. and Karissa rustling out of bed. Fog shrouded my brain, half sleeping, half awaiting her to come say goodbye. There was a brief moment where I debated getting up and joining her at practice that morning. It was very brief, and I quickly dozed back off, only to awake once again for my goodbye kiss.

"Have fun at yoga," I murmured in a sleepy haze as she left.

She had been teaching at the local rec centre for a while, and like many other Friday mornings, she had to teach this morning. I opted to stay in bed and grab an extra hour of sleep, instead of joining Karissa for her morning yoga practice.

My alarm went off, forcibly removing me from my peaceful slumber at 7 a.m. I headed down to the kitchen, and like most mornings, I queued up some music. If Karissa had been there, we'd have battled for control of the selection — me with my Nickelback or AC/DC, her with Sara Barelles or Ed Sheeran. This morning I was on my own, so Iron Maiden helped me kickstart the day.

I looked at the clock. 7:08 a.m. She should have wrapped up yoga by then and would be getting ready to head home. The thought of her made me smile.

At 7:12, I texted her as per our usual morning routine. "Morning!"

No response.

Perhaps she had gotten caught up with one of her students. Karissa certainly enjoyed being with them, and it was not uncommon for her to become engaged in long conversations. She was the type of person who would gladly be an ear for anyone who needed it, so it was quite plausible for her to be sitting around with a student, listening to their latest life drama. She had an uncanny knack for making you feel better simply with her presence.

The thought reminded me of when she first took me climbing, how we would do a lap and then sit and rest, letting our arms recover for the next lap. I always felt the need to get back on the wall ASAP. She would gently pull me down onto the mat and whisper, "Relax, there's no rush." We would then sit in comfortable silence.

I carried on with my morning routine, rocking out to some Nickelback, free from the menace of Ron Pope's guitar licks, preparing breakfast, showering, and dressing for my day. It was a day I was looking forward to: I had some prospective new recruits for our business, a meeting with my divorce lawyer to hopefully finalize that chapter of my life, and an open evening that Karissa and I had not yet decided how to spend together.

7:48 a.m.: "How was Yoga?"

No response.

Karissa and I were very thoughtful with our texts, always careful to sign off rather than simply disappear, always considerate about letting the other know what we were up to. This was feeling a little out of character, and I started wondering if I had done something that had upset her.

There was no rational thought behind this. We had had a wonderful evening together the previous night, but you know how that inner chatter in your head works. It starts filling in the blanks with mindless negative drivel. I could feel a little bit of anxiety creeping in, and I didn't like it at all.

Our relationship was solid. There most certainly would be a valid reason for the radio silence.

I left the house, and after a quick stop at the office, I headed downtown to my lawyer's office to see what kind of progress we could make.

I checked my phone. Still no response.

Now my head really started going places. Her ex-husband had asked if they could get together for a coffee earlier that week. She mentioned to me that it was a bit of an odd request and seemed quite formal.

Perhaps she had taken him up on the request this morning and had met him for a coffee. Were they getting back together? Oh man, that useless chatter was starting to run away on me.

My first meeting was done and still no response. This was very odd indeed. My head bounced back and forth between worry for her safety and worry of heartbreak. So I got a little more insistent.

10:06 a.m.: "Hellooooo!"

You know that sinking feeling you get when you get stood up by a loved one, even for a few minutes or hours? I was starting to feel that. I realized how much I relied on our little text banter for validation of our relationship, and how much I disliked it when that routine was broken.

I headed back to the office. My next meeting was at 11 a.m., and I couldn't get my mind off Karissa. Where was she? Was she okay? Had there been an accident? Was she with her ex-husband? Karissa also had an ex-boyfriend that had been particularly difficult to deal with. In fact, she had filed a restraining order against him. But he hadn't shown his face in months.

10:17 a.m.: "Your silence worries me. Let me know you are OK please."

By this time, I was starting to get legitimately concerned. I'm honestly not much of a worrier, but something just did not feel right. I tried to carry on as normal. My 11 a.m. was with two prospective new recruits to whom I had been talking for quite some time, and they were finally coming into the office to have a serious discussion about the possibility of joining our team.

I should have been on cloud nine prepping for the meeting to finalize the "sale." Instead, there was a knot in the pit of my stomach that shrouded everything.

10:59 a.m.: "Hey. My 11 o'clock is here but I really worry about you with your nutty ex. Hopefully you're just busy but let me know you're ok. {kissy face emoji}"

With still no answer from Karissa, my stomach was in knots. I can feel it now, even as I describe this. Breath shallow, dread in my heart, that feeling that something just isn't right. Not only was my mind playing games with me, but now my body was as well. I was starting to feel physically ill.

This 11 a.m. was an important meeting, not one for which I wanted to be distracted, but I was having a hell of a time concentrating. There were two people coming in for the meeting. The intent was to discuss our organization's offering, as well as give them a demo of our back-office software.

When I made my way into the boardroom and welcomed them, I pulled my cell phone out of my pocket and put it on the table. I made up some sort of excuse about one of my kids not feeling well and said

I needed to keep my phone accessible in the event that they called and needed assistance. I mean, who could ever fault a businessman for being an attentive father? Certainly, that felt more acceptable than, "I'm worried about my girlfriend because she hasn't texted me back this morning."

We started the meeting and had our typical back and forth, me answering the standard questions as if on autopilot.

Then my phone rang. My heart leapt. I picked it up and looked at the caller ID.

Blocked Number.

Crap, not Karissa.

I ignored it, and my mood went from instant relief to deeper anxiety. I tried hard to put my focus back on the meeting, but I'm fairly certain it was one of the poorer performances I've put up. I managed to muddle my way through, and eventually we all agreed to head across the street for lunch. I suggested bringing our VP of Operations with us so they could get a sense of who Connie was, as she would be their direct line of communication to me when they needed anything handled. Frankly, I was relieved to have some of the focus taken off me.

As we were about to be seated at the restaurant, my phone rang again and I nearly jumped out of my skin. I looked at the caller ID, which again read "Blocked Number."

This time I answered it.

The voice on the other end of the line asked if this was Mike Cameron, to which I said yes. He then went on to introduce himself as Constable So-and-So. I instantly forgot his name.

My heart sank, and I said, "Is she OK?"

He responded, "Where are you?"

"Is she OK!?"

"Where are you?"

I practically yelled, "IS. SHE. OK?"

He said, "Where are you? We're at your house. We're coming to you."

Finally, I told him where I was.

He said, "Stay right there. We'll be there in five minutes."

Connie followed me out the door. I told her who had called and asked her to take over the meeting and give the recruits my regrets.

As I waited for the constable to show up, my phone buzzed again, this time a text message from a number I did not recognize. The message was from a business friend who lived in the municipality where Karissa lived.

12:44 p.m.: "Mike, I hope all is well with you? I heard through small town gossip that your girlfriend may have been involved in an incident here this morning. I sure hope not. If it's true, my heart goes out to you and her family. Again, I hope it's not true and the rumour mill is flawed. Thinking of you."

I replied immediately. "Police are en route. I know nothing."

12:46 p.m.: "I hope all these vicious rumours are just rumours. Take care my friend."

What the fuck was going on?

My head was reeling, not wanting to come to terms with what might have happened. The day started to feel like an otherworldly experience.

It's incredible how your body can take you back in time. As I revisited this string of texts for the first time in order to write this scene, I could feel my body physically reacting the same way it had on that day — mind jumping all over the place, eyes unable to focus, breathing heavy, a large weight on my chest, augmented by a giant lump in my stomach.

Holy fuck, what the hell was happening? I kept thinking. *This cannot be my life.* There had to be some simple explanation for it all. My gut knew something terrible had happened, but my mind alternately tried to reject it and support a more favourable scenario. The cognitive dissonance racked my body, mind, and soul.

I stood outside the restaurant and started putting together the inevitable conclusion: the fucking bastard ex-boyfriend must have violated the restraining order and done something awful. My thoughts ping ponged from hoping for the best to expecting the worst.

Then the thought struck me: how did I know that was the police who had called me? What if it was him? What if he had plans for me? I thought to myself that I would have to make sure I asked the constable for ID when he arrived. Maybe this was really all a ploy to come after me, too. Or maybe she was just fine. But wait? What about the text from my friend?

An unmarked police car pulled up across the street, and two men hopped out. I started moving across the street toward the driver. I remember scanning the vehicle, then taking in his countenance, the thought of asking for ID still playing at the edge of my mind but starting to seem less necessary now. The vehicle was clearly an unmarked police car. The man approaching me, while not in uniform, was fit, strong, and wearing a badge on a lanyard around his neck and what movies would lead me to believe was a Glock on his hip. There was really no mistaking this man for anything other than a police officer.

While I was taking him in, he asked if I was Mike Cameron. I grunted some kind of confirmation as I looked up and found his eyes cold and hard. He just looked at me and stated three words that would change my life forever.

"Karissa is dead."

I was stunned. This could not be real. My heart sank.

I know that you might expect me to use a cliché — "I felt like I was hit with a 10-tonne truck," or "It felt like I had been hit by a freight train." The reality is, I don't think I felt. At all. I was numb. In complete disbelief, my mind and body were unwilling to accept this simple truth the officer had so bluntly stated.

The rest is a bit of a blur.

I think I asked him, "Was it him?"

He didn't answer but instead asked me to come sit in the back of the vehicle.

Eventually the interrogation ended. One of the constables handed me a business card and started giving me what I can only imagine was a well-rehearsed and far too often performed speech.

"... and on the back of the card is the number for victim services."

I think that's when I came out of movie mode. Up until then, all I could think was that this kind of thing doesn't happen in real life. Things like this only happened in the movies. That mantra had been playing in my mind through the entire interrogation. I must have said the phrase "This can't be real" at least a dozen times in between their questions.

Somehow the introduction of victim services made it concrete. The little 3.5" x 2" piece of paper that I now held in my hand somehow crystalized all of the things I had been told so far. In that moment, it all became real for me.

I still really had no idea what had happened, and the officers refused to tell me anything. They offered to take me somewhere, so I asked them to take me back to my office. The constable questioned that choice and suggested that perhaps they could take me to a family member somewhere instead. I told them that my work family was exactly who I needed to be with and that they would take care of me.

Then it hit me. Was he still out there? Was her ex-boyfriend still on the loose?

I asked them, "Should I be concerned about the safety of our kids? Should I be concerned about my safety?"

While still not really telling me anything, the driver said something to the effect of, "We're not actively pursuing anyone in this investigation."

I could not wrap my mind around what he was saying. I was getting frustrated while trying to be tolerant of these two guys doing their job.

"I feel like I am not asking you the right questions," I said, sensing that they were trying to tell me something while still staying duty-bound to whatever confidentiality was required.

"Let me put it this way," the first constable said. "If there were any one around to pursue, we would be actively pursuing them. And when I say 'around,' I don't mean that they have left town, because for an incident like this, we would pursue them no matter where they went."

Only when he said those words did I realize what must have happened. Only then did I realize the ex must have also taken his own life, though the officers wouldn't confirm what must have transpired. It was an odd feeling to be so devastated by the loss of Karissa's life, and then to feel relief at the loss of another.

By this time, we were in the parking lot of my office. I got out, still holding the business card with the victim services information on it. I walked into the office where Connie and the rest of the staff waited for me. She put her arm around me, and I said, "She's dead." I remember bursting into tears and shouting, "I don't even know what to do!" I threw my phone on the ground and crumpled down to join it there.

Connie put her hand on my back and said, "That's okay. You don't need to know what to do."

When I finally made it to my office and called my parents, I tried to keep my composure long enough to tell Mom what had happened. She had just spent a few days with Karissa and me about a month earlier.

"Karissa is dead," I told her through sobs.

How many more times would I have to say those words? To this day they still cut like a knife, tearing through my heart and reminding me of the loss of the most beautiful woman I have ever met.

Mom and Dad agreed to come out on Monday to stay for a while.

Most of the rest of that day is a haze. There are bits and pieces I remember — odd, meaningful moments in an otherwise senseless day. Some of my staff took me across the street to the park where we hung out in the sun. I remember there being some talk of yoga, but I don't know if I practiced any. I suspect that they were all just trying to provide some kind of distraction, some kind of escape from the inescapable.

One of my agents, Renee, called to ask my permission to share my contact info with Karissa's sibling's husband. Apparently, Karissa's ex-husband was trying to get ahold of me. I assured her gratefully that of course she could share my contact info. There was nothing more that I wanted in that moment than to be connected with some piece of Karissa, with those who knew her and had loved her, whether it was a brother-in-law, her ex-husband, or her children.

God, her children. When would I see them? How would I face them? How could these circumstances come to be the first time I would meet them? Karissa and I had signed up for an improv class that her oldest daughter was to attend with us. Would she still consider going?

My work friends and I went to sit on the patio back at the restaurant where I had first heard the news. I reminisced about a photo session that Karissa and I had done on that very spot. On the very couch on which I sat, in fact. Although each memory provided brief consolation, they could not insulate me from the overwhelming tsunami of my grief.

It was there that I finally received a phone call from her former husband. However awkward this introduction, at that moment I was incredibly grateful to be included. He told me that the family was meeting at his house and gave me the address. I told my team that they could go home, that I was going to go join the family.

Grief is a funny thing. Everyone seems to try and claim their space in the deceased's life. I desperately wanted to be part of the family mourning this woman, for whom we all shared a common love. The thought of grieving alone felt unbearable.

When I arrived and walked toward the door, there were people milling about out front, none of whom I recognized. Then Karissa's 16-year-old daughter spotted me and headed towards me. I wrapped my arms around her and immediately fell apart.

I felt completely useless. My heart ached for her. What can you possibly say or do for a young woman who just lost her mother? She had an odd sense of strength about her as I held her and I balled my eyes out.

"I'm sorry," I finally said. "It's us adults who are supposed to be the strong ones."

"I thought I was going to have to wait until improv to see you."

"Are we still going to go?"

"I sure as hell am."

Thinking that I would still get the chance to know this beautiful young woman whom Karissa adored gave me a great deal of comfort. She was certainly showing more composure than I was at that point.

The mood was sombre in that house. I was in a room full of strangers who were now family through circumstance. I met siblings and relatives I had not met before and certainly was having a hard time keeping names straight in my head. Her oldest son held me the longest of all, clearly a young man lost and in need of connection. We were two of a kind that afternoon.

The youngest children were not yet home and did not know what had happened. An uncle had been sent to pick them up. I was utterly destroyed thinking of the prospect of their having to learn that their mother was gone.

My god, she was gone. It hit me again, the crushing weight becoming more real with each passing moment, with each new relative showing up, reconfirming the most unreal of realities.

I will never forget the look on her youngest daughter's face as she got out of the car, looking at all the people milling about her father's front lawn and on his porch step. Her father went out to escort her inside. Her look of bewilderment turned to terror, as she must have realized something awful had happened to draw such a crowd. She likely realized at the same time that her mother was the only one not present.

I weep for her loss as I recount the scene. It is by far the most indelible picture etched in my memory for all time. Shortly after, I watched Karissa's young son being led upstairs to learn the news. I cannot even venture to imagine what type of scarring such news must leave on a young mind.

With nowhere to go and no idea what to do, I stood in the kitchen quietly watching the scenes of the day unfold again and again in my mind's eye, still trying to will myself out of this nightmare. Reality refused to take hold. I was relieved when her oldest son asked me to take him to the convenience store to buy some smokes. It was a relief to spend some time with him away from the madness of the house and to focus on something as normal as a trip to the store. Back at the house, as time passed, I felt more and more awkward as the kids dissipated and family started leaving.

Time has made a blur of the memory, but eventually I ended up at a local restaurant/bar where some of my work colleagues had gone. Jen, a friend of Karissa's whom I was just getting to know, joined us. We sat there for several hours drinking and telling Karissa stories.

It was pretty amazing, now that I think about it. There was lots of laughter, with Jen doing her best Karissa impression, imitating the distinctive nuances of the woman we had lost. We told story after story. I learned from Jen how much some of the things that I had done for Karissa had meant to her. It warmed my heart. We were laughing at the memories and crying for the woman we had lost. Drinking to forget the current reality.

Trying, one more time, to will it all away.

WHEN SOMETHING'S GOTTA CHANGE:

There simply are no words to do justice to this chapter. No questions I could ask of you powerful enough. So instead I would ask that we use this chapter to practice empathy.

How are you feeling right now?

____

____

____

____

How would you feel if you were in my place that day?

____

____

____

____

CHAPTER 29

GRIEF

Waking up the day after Karissa's murder, trying to shake off the cobwebs, I was still completely at a loss. Life had changed forever. The woman who had changed me was gone.

I had no idea what to do, but I knew I needed to keep myself active somehow. So I started putting together a video montage of some of our photos together. It was all I had left — a series of photographs and a heart full of memories put together in an impossibly short five months with her. All I wanted was to share her. What I really wanted was to bring her back, but since that wasn't going to happen, I wanted the world to know what they had lost.

It was at an Ed Sheeran concert I took her to that I first started to acknowledge the depth of feeling I had for Karissa. His song "Photograph" seemed perfect for the video montage. Absorbing the lyrics, I let them wash over me and take me away from the cold hard reality of my world. I played the song on repeat while I worked to choose the photos with which I most connected.

I thought back to less than a month before, when we had traded lyrics via text from opposite sides of the country. I had been at a Mortgage Professionals Canada board meeting hosted in Halifax, Nova Scotia, and Karissa was back home. With board meetings done for the day, some of the team went to explore the local establishments. Karissa and I exchanged texts in between my conversations with my group.

One of the things I loved was the openness of our conversations. We had some great discussions around making the other feel comfortable in our absence when out on the town. I shut down relatively early, a few beers in, and retired back to the hotel. Karissa told me on a few occasions that she liked it when I had a few beers in me. When I asked why, she told me that I was much more open, that at other times I was emotionally guarded. Anyway, this particular banter lead to us exchanging Ed Sheeran lyrics.

Me: "You can fit me"

Her: "Inside the necklace you got when you were sixteen"

Me: "Next to your heartbeat where I should be"

Her: "Keep it deep within your soul"

At the time, it was a playful exchange. Now the texts felt much more meaningful, resonating loudly on this day. All I had left were memories and photographs, and the images were something that I could share.

I compiled the video, uploaded it to my own website, and made it available via a link that I posted on every platform I possibly could.

On both Friday and Saturday, I fielded a number of inquiries from the media wanting to talk to me about what had happened.

I could not stand the thought of them sensationalizing what had happened, nor could I stand the thought of her murderer getting any attention whatsoever. I ended up speaking with Global News and expressing my concerns. The reporter assured me that her intent was to memorialize Karissa and share her story. I agreed to meet with the reporter and her camera crew at my house Sunday morning.

One of the most difficult things in the aftermath of a tragedy is that well-meaning friends want to help and will say things like, "If there is anything I can do, let me know." This is great, except that usually the person you wish to assist has no fucking idea what you can do to help, and actually trying to figure out how you can help can add to the stress.

Fortunately, I have some pretty amazing colleagues I'm proud to call friends. One texted me that evening and said, "We're coming over tomorrow morning with coffee and croissants. We'll see you at 11." The memory still makes me smile. I'm not certain they know how much that meant to me at the time. So about an hour before the reporter and her camera crew showed up, so did my reinforcements.

I was grieving, but I wasn't alone. I had people who loved me and knew how to show it. When it comes to grieving, regret is one of the most painful parts.

After Karissa was murdered, a feeling of despair overtook me, and a lens of pointlessness shrouded my world for a time. I could have tried to avoid it, to smooth over it with alcohol or other temporary fixes. I understood those temptations.

People told me, "Be strong." I loved them for their intentions, but I was saddened by our western culture. There can be no strength without weakness. If ever there was a time to be weak, this was it. Ultimately, I had to make the choice to endure the pain in order to come out a better man on the other side. Examining, absorbing, and enduring what I felt allowed me to grow substantially.

Sometimes I would curl into a ball and weep softly; other times I would wail loudly, cycling through grief and anger, beating my hands violently on my steering wheel while driving. I would let the emotions envelop me completely, simply observing them. I think this allowed me to detach, so as not to become completely overwhelmed, while still letting the emotions flow.

I've learned more from these moments than from anything else in my life. The hardest and yet the most important thing for me while grieving is to stay open.

I did at times find solace in sharing with others, but at other times I found myself frustrated with well-meaning individuals who simply did not, and likely never would, fully understand, at least not be able to empathize. Being able to feel what others feel gives you the greatest insight into who they are and allows you to find ways to make the greatest impact in their lives. While this lack of empathy was a source of frustration then, I am comforted now that I can use what I went through to empathize and help others in similar situations through their own grief.

After the death of a young girl, the spiritual teacher Ram Dass wrote a letter to her parents. "Who among us is strong enough to remain conscious through such teachings as you are receiving?" he asked. "Probably very few."

"Sometimes in order to keep it together you need to lose your shit."

I have remained conscious through my grief. While this was not an experience I would wish upon my worst enemy, Karissa's death was an opportunity very few are afforded. I needed to be strong enough to receive the lessons. When I couldn't be strong, I retreated into my yoga practice.

Finding something spiritual to grab onto helped immensely. The only way through was to have faith in what was on the other side.

A good friend of mine, Drew Dudley, said, "Just about everything awesome is on the other side of something shitty."

Two days after Karissa died, I was standing in the parking lot with Drew, saying goodbye. He hugged me and said, "Keep it together."

I replied, "Nope, I'm going to go home and lose my shit."

He looked at me, cocked his head, and said, "Don't confuse the two. Sometimes in order to keep it together, you need to lose your shit."

One of the things that I find frustrating is how we — and here I mean Western society or culture — define the word "strong" when it comes to grieving. Somehow, we have come to the conclusion that strength means fighting how we feel. We wage a war on our emotions and we go into battle. We never let our emotions bubble up to the surface. If we do, we are seen as weak, less than.

This is especially true as a man.

As men, we're discouraged from showing our emotions. We're taught to suppress, deny, and try to ignore negative feelings under the guise of being strong. It seems like such an oversimplification to say the key is *allowing yourself to feel*. The truth is, that simple message is the lesson for this entire book. If you take away nothing else from this time with me, I want you to take away this: it is okay not to be okay.

The key is allowing yourself to feel all of it.

We don't have to put up a facade, a mask, which we do for the benefit of others, anyway, and not ourselves. Feeling is one of the most courageous things we can do. It's not easy to allow your emotions to come to the surface. We tend to think that if we simply push them down, they'll eventually dissipate. This is not usually the case. Our bodies have a way of getting these feelings out one way or another. If we suppress and ignore, we may get physically ill. We may have breakdowns at inopportune moments. For each of us, repressed grief can manifest itself in a variety of different ways. One thing I know for certain is that it *will* manifest.

I found it really interesting that, as public as my grieving was, I would have many people come to me and share with me their stories of grief. Almost without fail, they would qualify their stories: "I know this is nothing compared to what you went through..." I'm not sure why we as humans feel the need to compare our struggles.

Grief comes in so many different forms. It's not always about the loss of a loved one. Grief can come with any kind of loss. Whether we're talking about a horrific tragedy or the loss of a job, a friendship, a marriage—it's all grief. The process is the same, and there's no need to compare the magnitude of the event you're grieving. For me, it was comforting to remember that we all struggle. All of our struggles are different. Most importantly, I remembered that we don't have to struggle alone.

There is no right way to grieve. Only your way. People will try and tell you the right way. Nod and acknowledge but find your own intuitive way. There is also no time frame for grief. I moved through, and continue to move through, my emotions because I did not — *do* not—fight them.

Even the sadness has become a friend. Sometimes I will weep alone, holding Karissa in my mind. People ask, "Don't you find that painful?" No, it's more like having a coffee with an old friend.

From the start, I swore that Karissa's story would not end with her life, that I would continue to ensure her legacy lived on. I carry her with me daily. I resurrect her in my memory as often as I can. A song, a smell, a view, a memory, or a conscious tug on my ear lobe like she used to do affectionately brings her to life for a fleeting moment. Not a day goes by that she is not still alive within me. Whether this helps or hinders my grieving process, it's the choice I've made.

Now, as I look back at that time in my life, at that horrific grief, I know that it made me stronger. Allowing myself to be weak didn't make me weaker. It tapped into something inside me that continues to make me more resilient.

The next step was figuring out what to do now that Karissa was gone.

WHEN SOMETHING'S GOTTA CHANGE:

Grief is deeply personal and is not limited to the loss of a loved one. It is an important process in our lives no matter what we are grieving.

What events in your life have caused you pain that you still need to grieve?

____

____

____

____

How do you allow yourself to grieve the losses in your life?

____

____

____

____

CHAPTER 30

FORGIVENESS

What has to be happening in someone's mind that can allow them to take the life of another? What twisted, mixed up reality do you have to be living in, to do something like that to another human being? What kind of misguided notion of what it means to be a man do you have to have to believe that two lives must end because you cannot "possess" someone you desire? For me, these are the questions that remained as I wrestled with the disdain for Karissa's murderer in my heart. I was angry, I was enraged, I was furious at this man who had taken away a partner from me, a woman who was a mother, a friend, and a wonderful human being.

When my wife and I split up after 13 years of marriage, two children, and 15 years together, we had to tell Chris and Mikaela the news. I will never forget the soul-crushing experience, me cuddled up with my son on our nest chair, Christine on the couch with my daughter. As I explained that Daddy was going to go live somewhere else for a while because we could not get along under the same roof, my son started softly sobbing while I held him in my arms. I continued to do my best to explain what was happening. How are a 12-year-old and a 10-year-old supposed to understand adult problems? I knew in that moment that this would be the most difficult thing I ever had to do in my life.

I was wrong.

Karissa's murder was the work of an individual who was not connected with, or in control of, his emotions. I had been introduced to what I thought of as a malevolent evil, a demonic presence with no regard for human life. A man who would take the life of the woman I loved. A man who would take his own life so that he did not have to face the consequences of his actions.

We make decisions based on emotion, justified by logic. This was a man who had made a decision with very permanent consequences based on a very temporary emotion.

I was certain of one thing: I could never hope to understand a man so vile.

In the wake of this horrific murder of a woman who still had so much to give to this world, her children, and society, I am faced with questions about how I feel about the system that failed Karissa. Could her death have been prevented by a society that actually teaches, respects, and values virtues like empathy and compassion and kindness over domination, conquest, and victory? How did our societal propensity to encourage unhealthy masculinities contribute to this event? How do we stop men perpetuating violence against women? How do we build a better restraining order? How do we improve the justice system to protect people like Karissa who so desperately needed it?

All of these are valid questions that need answers. It seems to me that tackling questions related to improving the justice system is akin to putting a band-aid on a ruptured jugular. We need to address the root cause and not simply build a bigger band-aid.

How do we prevent men from getting to this point in their lives where they can commit these atrocities? One of the most important things we can do to achieve this long term and for generations to come is to teach men to examine their tender sides, to explore and connect with their emotions without fear of vilification by their counterparts or, worse, their partners.

We need more men who will speak up and embrace compassion, empathy, and kindness. We need men to show the world that a combination of these characteristics helps to embody what it means to be a "real man."

Shortly after Karissa was murdered, I was directed to a parable, a story called "The Little Soul and the Sun," from three different sources. If there is one thing I have learned through all of this is that when the universe speaks, you should listen. So I did:

A little soul approaches God, excited to tell God that he "knows who he is." God asks, "Who are you?" The little soul goes on to say, "I am the light."

God concurs. Soon after, though, the little soul realizes that knowing who he is is not enough. He wants to *be* who he is. He wants to feel what it is like to be the light.

God explains that the only way for the little soul to know what it feels like to be the light is for God to surround him with darkness. There is no light without dark, no up without down, no warm without cold, says God. In order to experience anything, the exact opposite must exist.

Being "The Light" is very special, God goes on, explaining that it is okay for the little soul to shine his light through the darkness — and it is okay to be special, so long as the little soul keeps in mind that "special" doesn't mean "better."

God asks the little soul what part of "special" he would like to be. After some thoughtful deliberation, the little soul declares that he wants to be "forgiveness."

"That's wonderful," God says. "There's only one problem. There is no one to forgive. I made everything perfect."

Then the little soul realizes a large crowd of souls has gathered around to listen to the conversation. When he looks around at all the beautiful souls, he realizes God is right. They are all perfect. The little soul feels sad; he will never be able to experience forgiveness.

Then a friendly soul speaks up. "I will help you."

"How will you do that?" the little soul asks.

"I will come to you in the next lifetime and give you someone to forgive."

When the little soul realizes that the friendly soul will have to give up perfection in order to do something forgivable, he asks why the friendly soul will do that.

"Because I love you. I do, however, need you to promise me one thing."

The little soul is so excited at the prospect of experiencing forgiveness that he shouts, "Of course, of course. Anything, just tell me!"

"Always remember who I am. Remember me in my perfection."

I am paraphrasing and do not do the parable justice at all, so please read it in its entirety. The work is *The Little Soul and Sun* by Neale Donald Walsch. As I read the story for the first time, and realized what it meant, I did feel like I had just been hit by the proverbial freight train. I sat there reading, tears streaming down my face, as the enormity of the task at hand hit me.

I had to do the unthinkable. I had to do the unimaginable.

I was now, for real, faced with the most difficult challenge of my life. I had to forgive the man who had killed Karissa. I had to forgive the man who, at the cost of the woman I loved, would teach me the hardest lesson in forgiveness I could imagine.

There is no doubt — through 20-plus years in business, a car accident that almost took my life, my failed marriage, a fraud scheme that almost bankrupted me and many I loved, and all other obstacles life had thrown my way — that this was by far the most onerous task I have ever been given.

If I was to have even a whisper of equanimity, any hope of lasting peace, then I needed to release my heart of the hatred that threatened to consume me.

So I did. I said the words, aloud, for myself:

"I forgive you."

Many will not understand this choice or may even criticize me for writing about this decision. I know, however, that everything I have ever learned, everything that Karissa and I ever shared, every discussion we ever had led me to this, helped me become the man I am today. The man who can forgive.

You see, as hard as this is, the truth is I am grateful. I am grateful that I get to be the light. I get to choose to be the light and not the dark, to be love and not hate. This is a crux in my life, a crossroad where I get to choose the kind of man I want to be. In a world where one cannot exist without another, I am glad that I get to represent good and not evil.

I will love you forever, Karissa. You will never leave my heart. I am grateful for what we had together. I am grateful for everything you have taught me, and for everything you continue to teach me. I am a better man for your presence and the world is a better place because you were in it.

WHEN SOMETHING'S GOTTA CHANGE:

Forgiveness has nothing to do with the indivual being forgiven. Many times they may not even know. It is about finding release so that we can make our way forward. Living our best life.

Is there an anger, a bitterness, or even a hatred you have refused to let go?

____

____

____

____

Who do you need to forgive in order to move forward?

____

____

____

____

CHAPTER 31

OF ALL THE WORDS

One of Karissa's favourite authors was Kurt Vonnegut. She talked about his work often. As I reflect on our time together, it strikes me how appropriate one of his most famous quotes from *Cat's Cradle* is: "Of all the words of mice and men, the saddest are 'It might have been.'"

I can assure you I have pondered those 15 words more times than I can count. "What if?" "If only…" "What might have been?" It is hard not to get caught up in the sentiment of these words, even three and a half years since Karissa's murder. These words still invoke a deep, emotional reaction every time I read them. In fact, I broke down telling this story to Shannin, this book's editor. It is impossible not to let my rational mind fight the reality of what happened, screaming at me, wondering what might have been.

Vonnegut's quote now serves as a reminder to me to do my best to ensure I will never say them in the context of my life. To guarantee that I will live a life of love. To make certain that I will not leave this world with regrets. I will, in the words of Lenny Kravitz, "let love rule."

As I have discussed elsewhere in this book, I have a choice in this matter. I can choose to allow hatred — or regret, anger, resentment — to fill my heart, or I can choose love.

On October 2, 2015, I swore that I would not let Karissa's story end there on her driveway. I vowed that I would find a way to remain conscious through the teachings I was receiving. I would find some method of turning pain into purpose. That vow is difficult to live up to, because I am not the most significantly affected by the death of Karissa — and yet, her death has had the most significant impact on my life of anything I've ever faced. I feel inextricably linked with her, the two of us now indistinguishable. The path that we had begun together was forged even stronger for me by her passing and by the manner of her death.

The message Karissa left behind for me is not one of hate, blame, rage, despair, animosity, resentment, or even sorrow. While these are all emotions I needed (or need) to move through, they are not what matters most. What matters most is love. We need to allow for these emotions in order to find love and forgiveness on the other side.

Karissa was a shining example of leadership when it came to love. That is a legacy I intend to carry on. As a lifelong student of leadership, I look at some of the principles of leadership to see to how we as human beings can lead with love. In their book *The Leadership Challenge*, Jim Kouzes and Barry Posner wrote of the five exemplary practices of leadership:

- Model the way
- Inspire a shared vision
- Challenge the process
- Enable others to act

- Encourage the heart

Modelling all five of the practices outlined above can be extremely difficult in a world that tends to put love very low on the scorecard of success. Perhaps we should move love closer to the top.

We hear *en vogue* platitudes about love all the time. Certainly in a business world built on the hypermasculine traits of being ruthless and relentless, love is seen as weakness and is typically avoided at all costs. And while companies are now starting to throw the words around as corporate buzzspeak, do they truly "lead with love?" I don't know. Will such behaviour be rewarded or will our competitors walk all over us? Is the cliché "nice guys finish last" one that rings true or can we take some risks and "'model the way?"

So the question remains: why do we not live like this? Why are we so afraid of living who we truly are?

I think back to Karissa and our first date and how, for years, I had explored the phrase "I love you." I grew up with a belief in the blissful existence of "The One," my soulmate, my perfect match, my true love, that one person who completed my heart's desire. The individual who would give me those tummy butterflies for the rest of my life.

"I Love You" is Bullshit.

When I started to realize that my marriage wasn't "it," I really started to question this notion. After my marriage finally dissolved and I was faced with the fact that my wife was not "The One" for me, nor was I "The One" for her, I was forced to tackle this question head on.

When I wrote suggesting we "Embrace the Suck," I talked about "The Suck" being temporary, that emotions are fleeting. They came and they went. The more we embraced and experienced the negative emotions, the faster they would dissipate. While adhering to this idea allows us to more easily get through setbacks in our lives, and although this notion is useful when it comes to dealing with adversity in our life, it becomes problematic when we use the same theory in the context of love.

This dilemma really had me stumped. Is there truly "The One" or is it simply "The Next One?"

Let's assume we agree on the concept of there being a soulmate out there for you, that there is, in fact, *one* soulmate. What happens when "The One" is taken away from you unexpectedly? Does this mean that you are done, doomed to never love again?

That, I refuse to believe.

So my conclusion thus far? Does this mean that we should love less? Should we become more guarded and careful with whom or how we love? I would argue that it means the exact opposite. That we should love *more*, not less.

I do, however, think that the phrase "I love you" on its own is, in a word, bullshit.

You see, I was married for 13 years and pretty much daily said "I love you" to Christine. I fear we live in a culture where we always look for the easy way out, where we're always looking for shortcuts and trying to find the path of least resistance. When it comes to my marriage, saying "I love you" to my ex-wife was the easy way out. Please don't misunderstand. I did a lot of things wrong that contributed to my marriage ending, but like any failure, I've tried hard to learn from those mistakes.

Love is the most powerful emotion in the universe. Why would we let ourselves take the easy way out? I want you to imagine this with me. If you have someone with whom you share romantic love, or if you have a child or beloved siblings, dear friends who are closer to you than family; think about how much you love them. How does that make you feel?

Now I want you to come with me to a world where the phrase "I love you" doesn't exist. Those three little words are meaningless — I've taken them away. What will you do now? Will your loved one know they're loved? Will they know it any more or less than they do now while you have those words in your vocabulary? What about your children? Your feelings haven't changed, but you don't have those three little words to use as your crutch. How would that change things?

Three days before Karissa was murdered, she stayed overnight at my house. I was fast asleep, but she got up at about 3 a.m., came over to my side of the bed, kissed me, and told me she was going to drive home, because she had not been able to sleep for a while and had to be home early, anyway.

I sat up, moved over to make room for her, and invited her to lie down for a minute, concerned that something was bothering her. She lay on her stomach beside me, and I gently rubbed her back, simply enjoying being with her. She eventually fell back asleep, and we finished the night together. She did not need to hear me say "I love you." She felt, sensed, and knew I loved her.

Our understanding that the words were unnecessary stretched further back in our relationship, back to the Skaha Bluffs in Penticton where I had taken her climbing after a gruelling triathlon. My body hurt but my soul sang as I drove the first leg of our 11-hour ride home. Out of the corner of my eye, I caught her gazing at me with that soft, gentle smile, her heart in her eyes. I looked over, caught her eye, and cocked an eyebrow with an inquisitive expression. She beamed, smiling widely.

"Don't think it's lost on me what you did yesterday," she said, her recognition that I had taken her climbing even though I was exhausted from a triathlon. She squeezed my hand and nuzzled her head into my shoulder as I put my eyes back on the road in front of me. My body melted and peace washed over me. I can assure you, her words and gestures announced "I love you" louder than any megaphone, PA system, or amplifier.

Earlier in our relationship, on Karissa's birthday, I had been a little stumped on what to get her. Karissa was a woman who did not value material things. Knowing that her primary passion was climbing, I set up a date for us to go to the indoor gym early in the afternoon, with later plans to go out for a nice dinner.

Because I was still relatively new to climbing at that time and didn't have my "belay check" at the local gym, she could take me up the wall, but I couldn't take her. So I decided to make a trip to the gym on my own and get belay checked without her knowing. When we arrived at the gym, she was resigned to "bouldering" (climbing low without a rope) and belaying me. Imagine her delight when we checked in and my profile popped up with a big green check mark beside BELAY on the system. A small gesture in some ways, but one that I know moved her. Once again, I told her how I felt without using any words whatsoever.

I could give you a number of other examples, but I think you get the point. If you need those three, specific words to convey the message of how you feel to those you love, then I fear you are going to have a problem. And maybe even a deep regret one day when you can't go back and say more than those three words can ever convey. I feel fortunate that I was able to experience love — love without words, that I had the opportunity to show love, not just speak it. I can at least take some solace in that fact.

While I suspect that "encourage the heart" is an obvious tie in from my leadership training, I am left the much more difficult task: to "'challenge the process" as Kouzes and Posner suggest. It is hard, it is painful but there are also grains of joy sprinkled within the sands of agony, joy in continuing to explore these concepts together as Karissa and I were prone to do.

The most courageous thing that we can do as human beings is to drop the mask of who we think the world wants us to be and stand together in raw, unhidden beauty, ugliness or pain, revealing the true nature of our souls. It is only when we rise up — naked, stripped bare, and vulnerable — that we can see ourselves for who we are, either accepting, or challenging and changing.

When I reflect on that quote I learned from Karissa — "Of all the words of mice and men, the saddest are 'It might have been'" — all I can do is continue to sift through the anguish, searching for ways to sow these seeds of love throughout the furrows I have created in my world.

WHEN SOMETHING'S GOTTA CHANGE:

When we consider how saying "I love you" is bullshit, the phrases "show me don't tell me" and "actions speak louder than words" come to mind. While many answers still elude me, and likely always will, I come back to the simple truism "more love, less hate." This is an incredibly uncomplicated concept on which we should easily come to a consensus.

Where in your life are you taking the easy way out?

____

____

____

____

Where can you show more love for those around you, rather than simply saying it?

____

____

____

____

CHAPTER 32

IT'S TIME TO WOMAN UP

A number of years ago, before I met Karissa, I was out for a beer with my friend Viv one night, and somehow we got onto the subject of "manning up." I talked about how I really try hard to explore and grow in all aspects of my life, and about how it is such a shame that men are heartily discouraged from exploring, let alone sharing, their feelings and emotions. While men are programmed from a very early age to hide our feelings, women are more likely to be encouraged to express and explore their emotions. It is culturally acceptable for a woman to display emotion, but far less acceptable for a man to do so.

As we talked, I brought up how unfortunate the term is. I joked that men really needed to learn to "woman up."

Three years after Karissa's death, this sentiment resonates with me even more profoundly. In my career, I pay a lot of attention to the subject of "emotional intelligence," self-awareness, and personal growth. As I started exploring the concept of "womaning up," I really saw strong potential applications of this concept for my own development.

While I am typically fairly good at sharing my thoughts and, to some extent, my feelings, there are still many times when I find myself not fully expressing my ideas or emotions for fear of feeling like I am not man enough. Being a strong, confident man is high on my list of "who I want to be." But what it really comes down to is revisiting the definition of what a "real man" is. I wrestle constantly with my failed marriage and wonder if I wasn't "man enough" to keep it together sometimes. Don't get me wrong, I am a much better father today than I ever have been, and I think the path we chose was truly best for our family. Putting masculinity into a different context becomes a key factor for reprogramming how men behave when it comes to our emotions.

Putting masculinity into a different context is the key factor.

One of the most powerful speakers I have ever seen in my life is Frank Abagnale of *Catch Me If You Can* fame. At a mortgage industry conference I attended, Frank told the remarkable story of his life and had the audience riveted with his unbelievable tales of fraud, deceit, and conning. At the end of his presentation, he brought the entire speech around to what he believed the definition of a "real man i" was. Frank argued that masculinity is not about the money or the positions or the degrees; it's not about what you accomplish or how successful you become. He said a real man is faithful. A real man loves his wife. A real man puts his children first in his life. If he has done nothing better than to be a good husband and a good father, said Abagnale, that's the best thing he could possibly say about his life. He wrapped up by reminding us, if we still had our mother and father, to give them a hug and kiss while we still could.

I do not come close to doing justice to the emotional connection Frank created in the room that day. In a room of about 2000 mortgage professionals, he received a standing ovation, and I can tell you there was not a dry eye in the house. The lobby after that speech was packed with men on their cell phones with wives, children, and parents. It was an absolutely unbelievably emotionally charged room and an afternoon I will never ever forget.

And yet, most of the men avoided making eye contact with one another. I didn't really think about it much at the time, but I imagine now the reason for our shyness was for the fear of being laughed at for our emotions, being told to "suck it up, princess."

So what do I think it means to "woman up?" While I am not an academic expert in psychology, twenty years of study and personal experience in this arena has led me to the following conclusions:

1. **Self-awareness** is the key to growth and personal development. We need to be aware of who we are and what we feel: the good, the bad, and the ugly. If we want to grow, we need to know where we are starting. With awareness comes choice.

   "Emotional Intelligence" is defined as the ability to observe, interpret, understand, and manage both our own emotions and the emotions of those around us. We have already discussed the fact that women, generally speaking, are better conditioned by society at being "in touch" with their emotions. If men make a conscious effort to better observe and analyze their own emotions, rather than simply suppressing them, they have better opportunities to manage those emotions as well and to apply those same techniques to others.

2. **Decisions are made based on emotion** justified by logic, a claim neuroscience supports. When Dr. Antonio Demasio studied patients who had had brain injuries that affected the area of the

> brain that generated emotions, he discovered that individuals who could not "feel" had a very difficult time making even the simplest of decisions. They could logically describe what they should be doing, but in practice had a very difficult time making daily decisions about even the simplest choices, like what to eat or wear.

Imagine if you could be actively engaged in assisting your spouse, partner, or children in managing and directing their emotions by changing the way you interact with them, based on a better understanding of what triggers their emotions and how they behave in a variety of emotional states.

What would your relationship with your kids look like in 12 months if you mastered this skill?

What would your relationship with your spouse look like a year from now if you could become proficient in this skill?

Apparently, it has taken my entire life for me to learn these truths. I experimented with my own versions of masculinity as a teen and then into adulthood, from trying to fill my man card with conquests like Frank and the boys of Eron, to feeling the need to build a business of my own.

When Karissa was murdered, many of the people in my life thought I might want to seek changes to the justice system that surely failed her. After all, she had done all the right things, filed the right paperwork, gotten the right protection order. But when I look at where I can make the most impact on this world, I realize that it is not seeking change within the justice system. I have an even greater opportunity to influence practices that will have a significant, positive effect on those who employ them. I realized that a better question to ask is how we prevent emotionally disconnected men like that from existing in the first place.

While what Karissa's murderer did is the extreme end of the

spectrum, the truth is that men everywhere are hurting. Suicide rates, depression, and loneliness are at epidemic levels. Centuries of emotional deconditioning have left men ill-equipped to live full versions of who they really are.

Couple the idea of decision-making with Emotional Intelligence, and you have a very compelling reason to "woman up" and reconnect with our emotional selves. Our lives are defined by the decisions that we make. The better we understand the reasons behind our decisions, the more deliberate we can be about those decisions. This is a critical element if we care to have a purposeful life.

If we do not understand the emotions that drive the decisions we make, we have zero chance of living a fully awakened existence.

EPILOGUE

WHEN SOMETHING'S GOTTA CHANGE, MAYBE IT'S YOU

After Karissa's murder, I had many amazing friends, co-workers, and even strangers surround me, hug me, pat me on the shoulder with their heads hung low, saying, "Something's gotta change."

For quite some time, this became my mantra. I would wake up in the morning, head to the sink to brush my teeth, look in the mirror, and reflect on those three words: "Something's gotta change." I would say it over and over and over in my head.

"Something's gotta change."

"Something's gotta change."

"Something's gotta change."

Then one morning I added three words to that mantra that really changed everything for me. I started looking in that mirror and saying, "Something's gotta change...maybe it's you!"

It's easy to look around at all the social ills of the world, shaking your head and making the "something's gotta change" statement. It is entirely something different to take ownership of the phrase and get out and do what you can to be that change.

In all of the philosophical conversations Karissa and I shared, my favourite was on the topic of talent. I asked her what she thought her talent was. She responded, "I make things beautiful," which she absolutely had a knack for doing. She very readily saw and captured the beauty in everything with her art.

She turned the question around and asked me what my talent was. I hemmed and hawed a little over this and ended up saying that I wasn't sure I had one specific talent. Not to take away from what I had, but I really felt that there wasn't any one thing at which I had ever been especially gifted. I asked her what she thought my talent was, and she said, "You have a much more useful talent."

"Oh? What's that?"

"You have the 'make shit happen' talent."

This made me smile. So there you have it. She "Made Things Beautiful" and I "Made Shit Happen." Together we were going to "Make Beautiful Shit Happen."

On October 2, 2015, I vowed that I would continue to make beautiful shit happen in Karissa's honour.

Take ownership when "something's gotta change." And do what you can to "make beautiful shit happen" in your life — whatever that means for you.

#makebeautifulshithappen

MUCH LOVE,
MIKE

Acknowledgements

This may be the hardest part for me to write. As you can tell there are so many individuals who have impacted me over my lifetime and I am incredibly thankful for all of you who have shaped my experience on this planet so far.

I need to take a moment and acknowledge my partner Michelle de Bruin who has had to endure many tellings of this story. I know this process has not always been easy for you. I am incredibly grateful for your continued love and support. I hope I live "I Love You" is bullshit with you every day and look forward to "forehead time" forever.

To my parents who have always supported and encouraged me no matter how stupid or rebelious I became. I love you guys. My children who always make me proud, I am so excited to watch you move into adulthood and blossom into the young man and woman you are meant to become. Christine I will always be grateful for the opportunity to raise two wonderful human beings together.

Thanks to my Aunt Carly for providing a home for this 16 year old rebel and to my Aunt Sharon who taught me what it really means to be a badass.

For my editor Shannin who was incredibly helpful, not only editing the manuscript but also coaching me through the procrastination monster that seems to live so large in my life.

Graham, Darren and Rick it has been an amazing ride and I am so happy we have so many memories to share.

There are so many people who have been direct and indirect mentors in my life and while I may not be able to list you all here please know you have had an integral role in shaping this book.

And last but not least to you. Thank you for joining me on my journey. I'd love to stay connected. http://mikecameron.ca/connect

About the Author

Mike Cameron is a Canadian writer, speaker, philanthropist, ultramarathoner and advocate against Gender Based Violence. Mike went from literally bagging shit to founding, building and running an award winning multi-million dollar business. As a sales and leadership authority, Mike has studied and spoken on the impact that emotion has on human behavior for more than two decades. He has worked with a variety of non profits and charities to pave the way for a violence free future. Today he designs programs to assist men to tap into their emotions in a real and authentic way using his Emotional Reconnection Practice.

Mike co-founded the Ignore No More Run For Respect to help engage men and boys in the gender equity conversation. His keynotes addressing the importance of emotional intelligence have been heard all across North America. His 2017 Tedx "The Way Men Think of Strong Is Wrong," urges society to help redefine what it means to be a badass.

Connect'd Men Inc.

In 2018 Mike founded an organization designed to create safe, peer led environments where men can practice the art of Emotional Reconnection. In these spaces men learn to S.O.A.R.

S low Down

O pen Up (Share)

A ccept (without judgment)

R econnect (with their emotional selves)

You can find out more about Connect'd Men at:

http://fb.me/connectdmen

Made in the USA
Middletown, DE
10 November 2019

78350639R00175